MAKING ADORABLE
Button·Jointed
Stuffed Animals

20 **STEP-BY-STEP PATTERNS**
to Create Posable Arms and Legs
on Toys Made with Recycled Wool

REBECCA RUTH ANDERSON

All photography courtesy of Rebecca Ruth Designs except for stock photos as follow:

Flaticon.com: Price tag icon made by Smashicons (price tag icon 8); Wissawa Khamsriwath (knitting icon 8); and Freepik (church icon 8).

Freepik.com: isidoro151 (chapter opener background and header banners 19–20, 22–28); Olga–spb (chapter opener background and header banners 29–30, 32–35); Terdpongvector (chapter opener backgrounds and header banners 36, 38–43, 57–58, 60–62); Freepik.com (chapter opener backgrounds and header banners 44, 46–51, 52, 54–56, 63–64, 66–69, 70, 72–73, 105–106, 108–111, 118, 120–123, 150, 152–159); Nenilkime (chapter opener background and header banners 92, 94–98); and Stephanie2212 (chapter opener background and header banners 99–100, 102–104).

Shutterstock.com: Gitanna (buttons 2); Mascha Tace (3); Evgeny Atamanenko (top left 9); Auhustsinovich (bottom right 9); Jenn Huls (top left 18); Nadezda Barkova (chapter opener background and header banners 74, 76–81); Shum-stock (chapter opener background and header banners 82, 84–91); Kaewta (chapter opener backgrounds and header banners 112, 114–117, 133–134, 136–141); Alenka Karabanova (chapter opener background and header banners 124, 126–132); Tono Balaguer (water 125); and LikaKinsky (chapter opener background and header banners 142, 144–149).

ISBN 978-1-56523-944-9

Library of Congress Cataloging-in-Publication Data

Names: Anderson, Rebecca Ruth, 1950- author.
Title: Making adorable button-jointed stuffed animals / Rebecca Ruth Anderson.
Description: Mount Joy, Pa. : Fox Chapel Publishing, [2018] | Includes index.

Identifiers: LCCN 2018018273 (print) | LCCN 2018024490 (ebook) | ISBN 9781607655459 (ebook) | ISBN 9781565239449
Subjects: LCSH: Stuffed animals (Toys) | Button craft.
Classification: LCC TT174.3 (ebook) | LCC TT174.3 .A537 2018 (print) | DDC 745.592/4--dc23
LC record available at https://lccn.loc.gov/2018018273

To learn more about the other great books from Fox Chapel Publishing, or to find a retailer near you, call toll-free 800-457-9112 or visit us at *www.FoxChapelPublishing.com*.

We are always looking for talented authors. To submit an idea, please send a brief inquiry to acquisitions@foxchapelpublishing.com.

Printed in Singapore
First printing

INTRODUCTION:
Upcycle Older Garments to Make New Toys

Wool is a wonderful fiber. It is durable, colorful, and soft. Just because a sweater or coat is a bit worse for wear or out of fashion doesn't mean it can't find a useful new life. The button-jointed toys in this book are ideal for reusing wool fabric that otherwise would be destined for the landfill. The result is a delightful menagerie great for play or display.

These toys are easy to sew by hand and compact enough to work on most anywhere. You'll find that the felted wool feels lovely as you stitch. Felted wool is thick, giving strength and structure to the figure. Once felted, a freshly cut edge won't unravel. Because the raw edges of all seams are to the outside, there's no need to go through the tedious process of turning things inside out before stuffing.

You can use knitted wool (from sweaters) or woven wool (from garments) to make animals. Knitted wool generally felts into a thicker fabric than woven wool and it makes larger animals. Knitted wool also has more stretch than woven wool so it makes rounder animals. This book will brief you on where to hunt for suitable wool, how to identify it, and how to felt it to just the right texture.

These animals are made from simple shapes that, once stitched, are joined to the body with buttons. The thread holding the buttons goes through the body, making moveable joints that allow you to pose the figure. Using vintage buttons will add a lot of interest to your animal. Each button can be different—but it's important to use the size required.

The wide variety of colors and patterns in wool will give your creativity full range. Add decorative stitching of a jazzy color and some unusual buttons and you'll have a one-of-a-kind toy that is sure to please.

Safety note: These animals are great gifts for kids, but reserve them for children above the age of three. Younger kids might pull off the buttons and put them in their mouth—a serious choking hazard.

Contents

Projects

19

44

70

99

124

29

36

44

52

57

63

74

82

92

105

112

118

133

142

150

Choosing Material for Projects

The projects in this book can be made from wool sweaters or coats. They can be found and felted, but if you prefer a specific color or pattern, you can buy wool felt, polar fleece, or knit your own yardage. Here are your options.

Different thicknesses of felted knitted wool

Wool and Felting

Knitted Wool

Sweaters felt beautifully and are ideal for making animals. They yield thick wool because the process of knitting makes the fabric of the sweater thicker than woven fabric. Knitted fabric has more stretch built into it than woven fabric does. Some wool felts thinner and can be sewn on a sewing machine. Heavier knits remain thick after felting and must be sewn by hand. For example, cable sweaters most often felt up too thick to make animals. Instead, you can use them to make terrific tote bags or throw pillow covers.

Sweaters are knitted wool; a coat is woven wool

Woven Wool

Woven wool fabric felts, too, but won't have the same amount of stretch and body as a knitted fabric. Animals made from felted woven wool can be sewn by machine and will be flatter. A coat is the only type of clothing made from woven wool that is thick enough for these projects. Winter coats are made with a great deal of fabric and the wool is much thicker. The challenge is to find a coat-weight wool in bright colors; that's where the thrill of the hunt comes in. By contrast, men's suits are too thin and have too many seams to yield large pieces for felting. More often than not, they have interfacing fused to the inside surfaces, which should be removed before felting. The amount of fabric harvested is too small an amount and too thin a weight to justify the work of felting.

When looking through clothing, check for interfacing fused to the back side of the wool. Unfortunately, this can sometimes be problematic to remove. Look under the lining for interfacing (see inset on page 7). If the lining isn't loose—making it possible to see the back of the fabric—look for a rip in the lining to peak through. Sometimes it is possible to feel the presence of interfacing through the thin layer of lining. Should you choose a coat with fused interfacing, you can usually pull it off before felting. If some glue remains on the fabric, the side with dots of interfacing glue can be placed to the inside of your stuffed animal.

Wool blankets would seem to be a good source of project material; however, they usually felt up too thick to use for animals. If you're looking for a specific color, you could purchase woven wool by the yard from a fabric or craft store. It is expensive but often a great way to find the color you want. Remember to look for coat-weight wool.

Nonwoven Wool

Available from a fabric or craft store, **nonwoven wool** has fibers that have been bonded and compressed by a machine. Most often, this kind of felt is not made of wool, although woolen craft felt is available. This fabric is not as soft as felted wool and has almost no stretch. Sew it with a sewing machine.

Polar Fleece

Available in many colors and patterns, **polar fleece** can be used and does not need to be felted. Polar fleece has a great deal of stretch. Choose the thickest weight of fleece you can find. Check that the cut edge is pleasing since the raw edges will show when your animal is complete. Sew animals of polar fleece on a sewing machine.

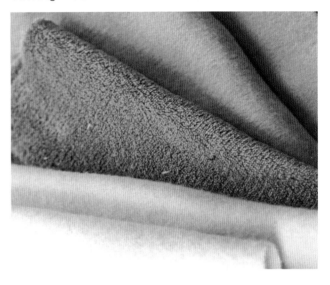

Hand-Knitted Wool

You can always make **knitted wool** yourself by knitting some yardage together with wool yarn. This will allow you to take advantage of the extensive color choices available. Knit twice the amount called for in the pattern—that way you will have plenty to work with after it shrinks in the felting process.

Where to Look for Wool

In your hunt for wool, search for 100% wool items. Many blends will work as well (80% wool and 20% other fibers) but 100% wool is best. Some wool, however, has been treated against shrinking during machine washing and will not felt correctly. It isn't always possible to know ahead of time if a garment will felt. A "dry clean only" tag is a good indication that it might work. Alpaca and cashmere have much finer/smaller scales than wool does and so is much more difficult to felt. I've never been able to felt either one, even after washing it six or eight times.

Since wool garments are made to dry clean, you can't be sure that the color is fast. Assume the dye may run and use a color fixative, like Retayne™, when you wash the garments.

Resale shops, thrift stores, and consignment shops are also good sources for wool.	Fabric stores can be good (if expensive) sources of coat-weight wool.	Search garage sales and bazaars at churches or other organizations.

EXAMPLES OF WHAT TO LOOK FOR ON THE LABEL

How Felting Works

It has happened to all of us. A beautiful wool sweater gets mixed into a load of wash. Even if the temperature setting was not on HOT, when we lift out the sweater at the end of the wash cycle, we see to our astonishment that it has shrunk to half its original size. And there is nothing we can do to reverse the damage.

That's the distressing side of felting. Intentional felting is a much happier process. It takes a loose material that will fray when cut and turns it into a super-strong fabric that cuts neatly without fraying. The felted wool's density means it has structure—ideal for making animal figures that can stand on their own four legs!

How felting works is pure magic resulting from the anatomy of each strand of wool. Wool is a protein fiber encased in tiny, overlapping scales. When exposed to hot water, the scales open. Agitate fiber against fiber and they latch onto each other. Once dry, the scales close, locking the fibers irreversibly. Wool will felt to thicknesses of 1/16" (1.6mm) to 3/8" (9.5mm).

How to Felt Wool

1. Before felting, cut off all buttons. Save them as options for joining the animal's limbs to their bodies.

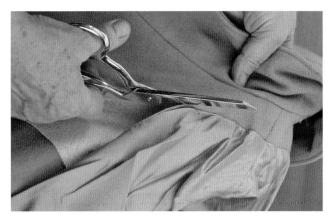

2. Remove all non-wool parts of the garment.

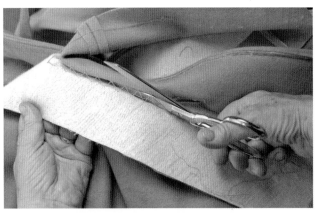

3. The collar and hem may be handstitched to the coat. They are easily cut away.

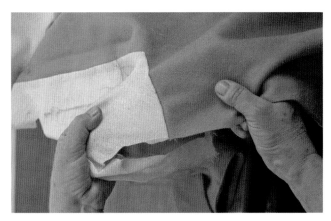

4. Pull off the interfacing. If it does not remove easily, you will have to cut it away. Expect to have less usable fabric as a result.

5. A harvested coat: the usable wool fabric is on the *left*, matching buttons are in the *center*, and on the *right*, the lining and interfacing that must be discarded.

6. Place items in pillow protector bags (to prevent any loose wool fibers from clogging the washing machine) and pin the zippers shut.

7. Wash similar color items in HOT water, using a mild detergent. Set a timer to reset the wash cycle. Ideally you should agitate the wool for 20 to 30 minutes. If you don't have a lot of wool to felt, add old towels or clean rags to the load.

8. After washing, examine each item to check that it has shrunk. You may need to run the wool through two or three wash cycles.

9. Dry the wool items in the dryer on hot or warm temperature. After drying, harvest the wool fibers from the filter to use in stuffing the animals.

10. Cut apart the garments along the seam lines. Cut off the seam allowance entirely—it's easier to press the wool without the bulge of the seam.

11. Press the wool flat with an iron set on the wool heat setting using steam.

THE RIGHT AND WRONG OF IT

Some knitted felt has a distinct right and wrong side. Even after felting you can see the knit and pearl stitches. Use the side you like the best on the outside.

Supplies

Use the best quality of supplies that you can afford. Good tools help make a project go smoothly.

Pattern Making

Photocopy or trace the pattern pieces for your animal using copy paper.

If you trace the patterns, use pattern paper instead of copy paper because it acts more like fabric. Use a fine-point marker to trace.

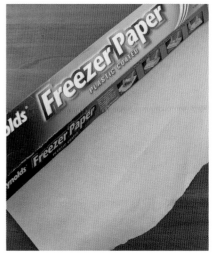

If you have thick wool, trace the patterns onto the non-shiny side of freezer paper. Press with a dry iron to adhere it to the wool before cutting.

Felting

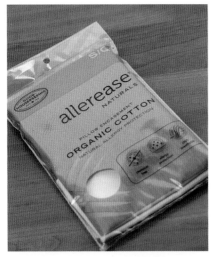

Use pillow protector bags during felting (to prevent any wool fibers from clogging the machine).

A needle-felting tool has barbs that push the roving curls into the wool. You can also get a holder for the tool for easy handling.

Upholstery foam makes a safe cushion to needle felt on. Inexpensive remnants can be found at upholstery shops.

Cutting and Sewing

Here are the cutting and sewing supplies you'll need to make the animals in this book. Many are items you probably already have in your basic sewing kit.

Straight pins are important. Heavyweight pins like craft pins are a good choice to hold the layers of wool as you work.

A pair of fabric shears is essential. Wool is thick, and good-quality, sharp scissors are important for proper cutting. A pair of small scissors for clipping thread is helpful as well. Since paper dulls scissor blades, you'll want a pair of good paper scissors to spare your shears.

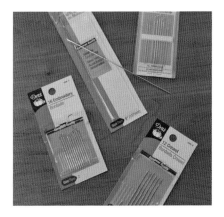

Use hand-sewing needles with large eyes for the heavy thread used with wool. Embroidery or crewel needles are a good choice. You also will need 5" (127mm)–long doll needles.

Thread Options

A 12-weight Aurifil™ thread is great for hand stitching. It comes in many colors. Use 40- or 50-weight thread in the sewing machine.

Pearl cotton is good for hand stitching and comes in many colors and weights. Use it to embroider features.

Buttonhole thread works well for hand stitching. It comes in a limited palette of basic colors.

Stuffing

Fill each piece of your animal firmly with stuffing. There are several options for stuffing, each of which gives a different feel to the finished piece. Put in small amounts at a time. Use a chopstick to push it in and manipulate the shape to what you want.

Wool roving is wool that has been cleaned and carded. The fibers are combed in one direction.

Polyester fiberfill is easily available and relatively inexpensive to stuff the toys. Cotton fill can also be found.

Wool scraps cut into small bits make good stuffing. It's a thrifty way to stuff an animal. Cut your scraps up small to prevent lumps.

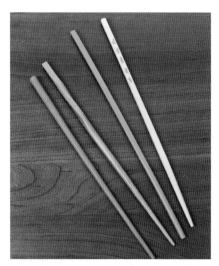

Use a chopstick or stuffing tool to push small pieces of stuffing into the animal parts.

Add polyester pellets to the bottom of the animals to give them weight and help them sit on their own. Use a funnel or rolled piece of paper to pour the pellets into the opening when stuffing.

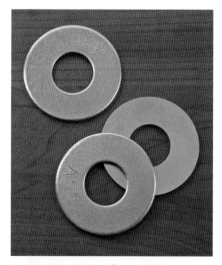

A metal washer from the hardware store placed at the bottom of an animal, like the hen, will help her sit and not roll. These are ¾" (20mm) flat washers.

Pattern and Sewing Techniques
Hand Stitching an Animal

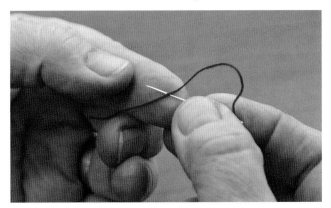

1. After threading the needle, pierce the short tail of the thread with the point of your needle.

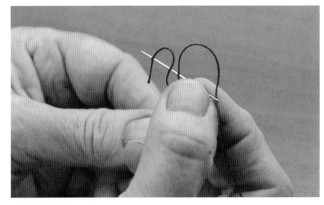

2. Pierce the thread with the point of your needle two more times.

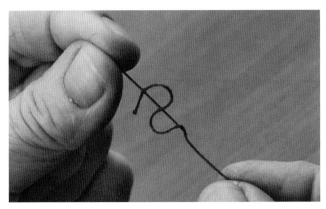

3. Pull the long end of the thread to slide the thread toward the eye of the needle.

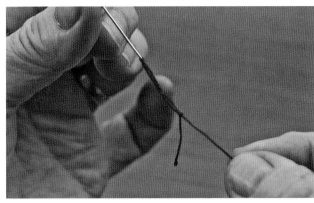

4. Slide the thread off the needle. The result: The interlocked thread will not pull out of the needle as you stitch!

5. Stitch ⅛" (3.18mm) from the edge. Pay attention to where you place the tip of your needle—this establishes your stitch length.

6. As you poke through the fabric, angle the needle back toward the last stitch.

DON'T FORGET BUTTONS!

When hunting for wool, also look for buttons for your animals. A variety of styles and colors is more interesting than ones that all match.

Save the buttons that you cut off the clothes you plan to felt. Coats have large buttons that match the fabric.

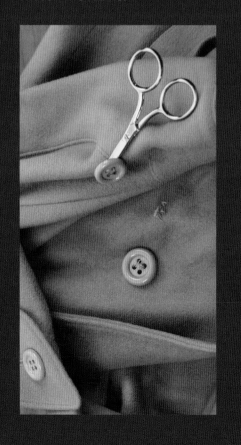

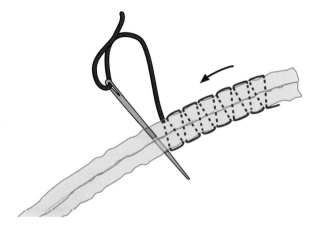

7. As you stitch, gently tighten the thread, pulling the pieces together. The stitches sink into the wool.

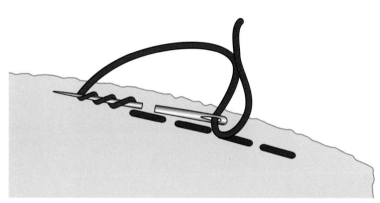

8. To make a knot, take a small stitch in the top layer of the wool. Wrap the thread around the tip of the needle three times.

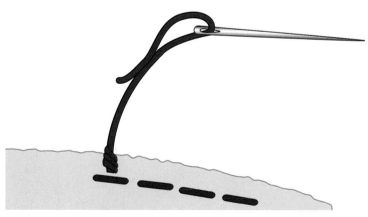

9. Pull the needle through, keeping the wrapped thread close to the fabric. Poke the needle through the fabric close to the knot to pull the knot into the wool. As you stitch, gently tighten the thread, pulling the pieces together. The stitches sink into the wool.

Machine Stitching an Animal

Sewing your animal by machine is quicker than hand stitching, but working with small seam allowances and thick wool can be tricky. Work slowly and carefully for success.

Attach a zipper foot on your sewing machine. Sew a scant ¼" (6mm) seam allowance.

If you are using thick wool, machine sewing can be difficult because the foot wants to fall off the thick layers. Try hand stitching thick wool instead.

PREPARING PATTERNS

The easiest way to prepare your patterns is to copy, print, and cut them out. If you plan to sew your animal by machine, cut out the pattern pieces a little larger to allow for a more generous seam allowance.

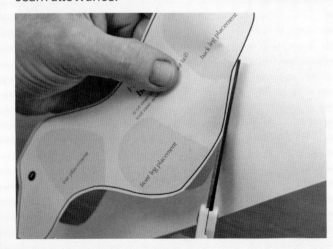

At the base of the foot, don't add extra for seam allowance. Simply cut out the pattern pieces along the lines.

Add extra space to the seam allowances

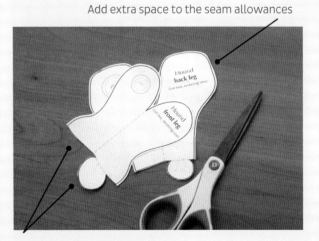

NO extra seam allowances at the bottom edge or base of the foot

Using Freezer Paper for Patterns

When pressed, freezer paper adheres to wool, eliminating the need to pin the pattern pieces to it before cutting. Here's how to use freezer paper with the Basic Dog pattern (see page 19) as an example.

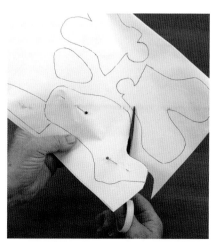

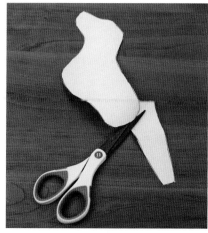

1. Cut out a 20" (50.8cm)–long piece of freezer paper, and trace the patterns onto the non-shiny side.

2. Fold the freezer paper in half and cut out the pattern pieces. This gives you the reversed shapes you need.

3. Cut off the tail section of *one* dog body pattern piece because you will only need one tail section attached to one side of the dog body.

4. Place the shiny side of each pattern toward the wool. Press them with a dry iron to lightly fuse the pattern onto the wool.

5. Cut around the freezer paper.

6. Peel the freezer paper off the wool.

THE BASIC DOG

Even you are not planning to make a dog, you'll want to read through this project. It will equip you with all the skills needed to make any of the animals—from transferring the pattern to positioning button-jointed legs just right. Once you grasp the skills needed, you can tackle the basics of any project in this book. If you ever find yourself lost while making one of the other projects, remember that you can always flip back to the Basic Dog project for a refresher.

This project will also introduce you to valuable techniques. You'll learn how to copy and trace the printed pattern provided with each animal and gain tips on how to accurately use them to cut the pieces that will make up your project. In addition, you'll learn the essentials of stitching and machine sewing felted wool, the art of stuffing, and how to assemble everything to make a beautiful little animal that you can pose.

The thickness of the wool you use will determine the size of your dog. My yellow dog was made from much thinner wool than my gray dog. Typically, I like to use a darker color of wool for the dog's ears. Using a variety of button styles and colors makes the dog more interesting.

SUPPLIES

- ¼ yd. (22.86cm) or 12" × 20" (30.5 × 50.8cm) felted wool fabric
- Buttons:
  - Two 1" to 1¼" (25 to 32mm) buttons, for back legs
  - Two ¾" to 1" (19 to 25mm) buttons, for front legs
  - Two ⅜" to ½" (10 to 13mm) buttons, for ears
  - Two ¼" (6mm) buttons, for eyes
- Large straight pins
- Large hand-sewing needle
- 5" (127mm) doll (soft sculpture) needle
- Quilting or buttonhole thread for hand stitching, or sewing thread for machine stitching
- Wool roving, polyester fiberfill, or wool scraps
- Chopstick or stuffing tool
- Freezer paper (optional)

Cutting out pattern pieces

1. Photocopy or trace the pattern pieces for the dog. Cut out the pattern pieces, using paper scissors.

2. If you plan to trace the patterns, do so on pattern paper instead of copy paper because it acts more like fabric.

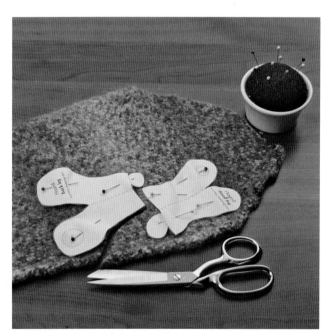

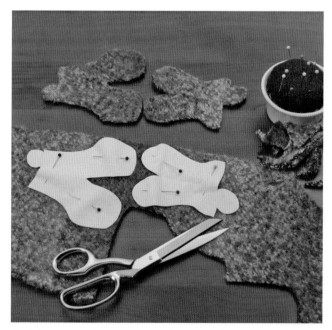

3. Pin the pattern pieces to a single layer of wool. Cut out each piece carefully, along the edge of the pattern piece.

4. Reverse the pattern pieces as instructed on each pattern piece and then cut out.

Sew the body

5. Fold the tail in half, with *wrong* sides facing. Pin the sides together.

6. Pin the body pieces together with *wrong* sides facing. Cover the base of the tail between the layers of the dog's body.

7. Stitch the tail and then continue around the body ⅛" (3.18mm) from the edge. Leave a 2" (5cm) opening for stuffing.

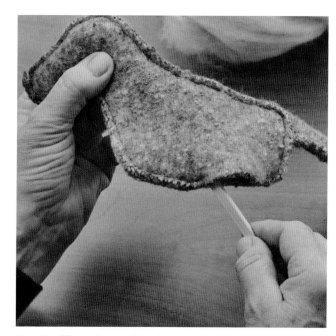

8. Stuff the body firmly, beginning with small pieces to fill the head. Use a chopstick to manipulate the shape.

9. When the body is filled firmly, shove the stuffing away from the seam line at the belly and pin the opening closed.

10. Stitch the opening closed. When done, manipulate the stuffing with your fingers to shape the body into a pleasing shape.

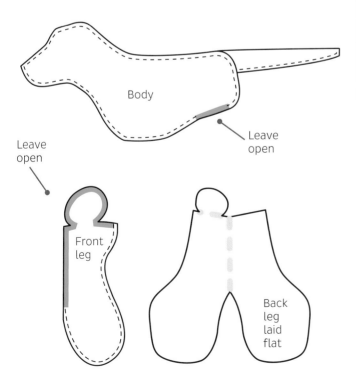

Body

Leave open

Leave open

Front leg

Back leg laid flat

11. Fold each leg in half with *wrong* sides facing, and pin.

Sew the legs

12. Stitch around the leg, leaving the foot open.

13. Fill the leg firmly with wool roving, polyester fiberfill, or wool scraps. Use a chopstick to push it in and manipulate the shape.

14. Fold the foot flap over the bottom of the foot. Hold it in place with one or two straight pins.

15. Hand stitch the toe and side of the foot flap to the leg. Leave the heel open.

Assemble the dog

16. Add filling to shape the foot nicely, then stitch the rest of the flap closed. Repeat for the other leg. Make the front legs in the same manner.

17. Use the doll needles as hinges to check the position of the legs. Pin the legs to the body using two pins in each. Pin the ears in place, too.

BUTTON POSITION CHANGES THE STANCE

You may need to re-sew the button joints. If the buttons are too high, the dog's legs will splay out; if they are too low, the dog will be knock-kneed.

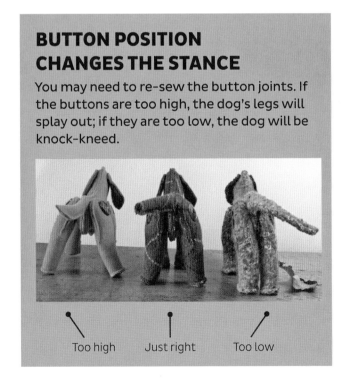

Too high   Just right   Too low

18. Check the position by standing the dog up and adjusting the leg positions as needed. I use black-headed straight pins to mark the eye positions.

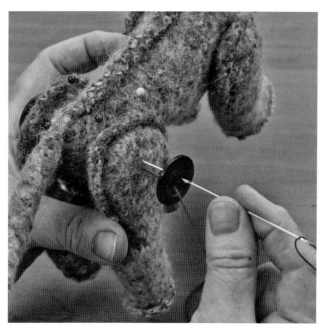

19. With a button on either side of the legs, sew through all layers with a doll needle and doubled heavy thread. Sew through the body and buttons multiple times to secure them.

20. Make a knot behind a button. Pull the loose end of the thread through the leg and cut it off close to the body.

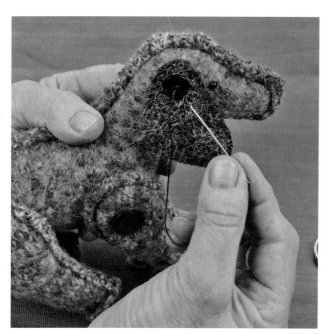

21. Position an ear in place on each side of the head; pin. Using a button on each side, stitch through the head to secure.

22. Sew ¼" (6mm)–diameter buttons in place for eyes. Stitch through the head, pulling the doubled thread to indent the head slightly.

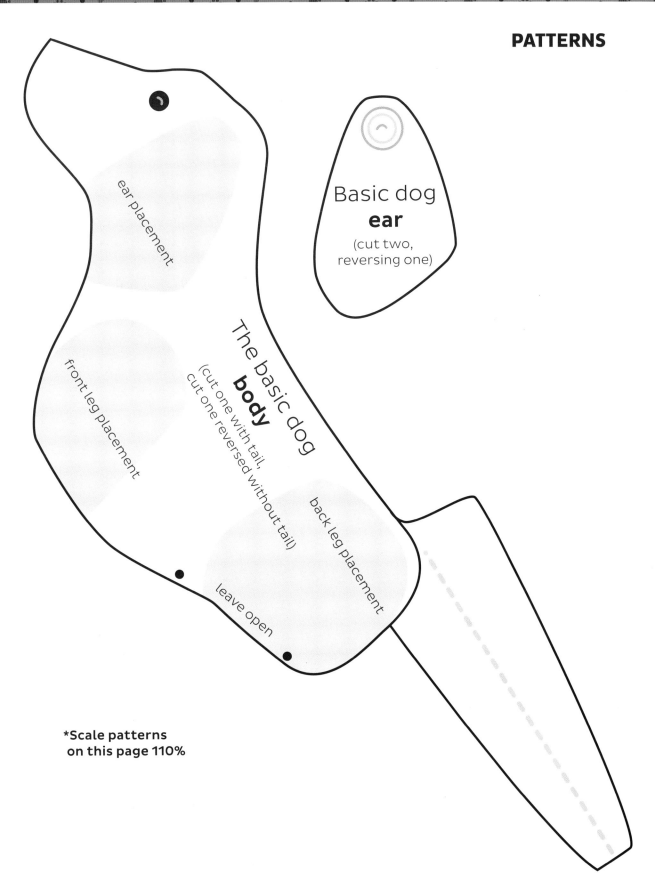

Basic dog
ear
(cut two,
reversing one)

ear placement

The basic dog
body
(cut one with tail,
cut one reversed without tail)

front leg placement

back leg placement

leave open

***Scale patterns
on this page 110%**

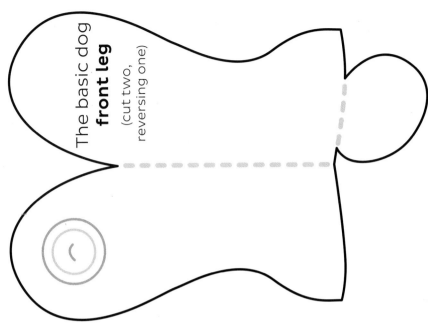

The basic dog
front leg
(cut two,
reversing one)

*Copy page at 100%

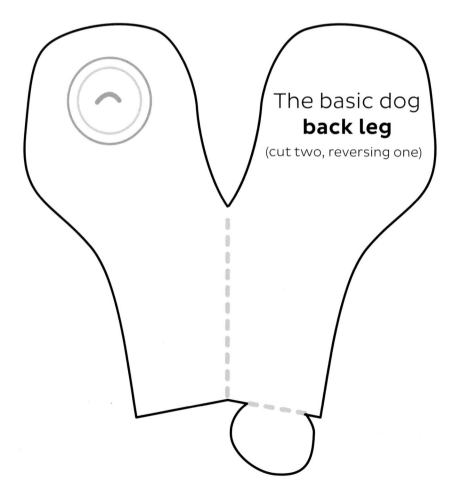

The basic dog
back leg
(cut two, reversing one)

WIRY TERRIER

The terrier is actually easier to make than the basic dog. The terrier's short tail is part of its body, so it doesn't need a separate step to complete. You can add whiskers and eyebrows with wool curls and a needle-felting tool to make a charming little guy.

SUPPLIES

- ¼ yd. (22.86cm) or 12" × 20" (30.5 × 50.8cm) felted wool fabric
- Buttons:
  - Two 1" to 1¼" (25 to 32mm) buttons, for back legs
  - Two ¾" to 1" (19 to 25mm) buttons, for front legs
  - Two ⅜" to ½" (10 to 13mm) buttons, for ears
  - Two ¼" (6mm) buttons, for eyes
- Large straight pins
- Large hand-sewing needle
- 5" (127mm) doll (soft sculpture) needle
- Quilting or buttonhole thread for hand stitching, or sewing thread for machine stitching
- Wool roving, polyester fiberfill, or wool scraps
- Chopstick or stuffing tool
- Freezer paper (optional)

1. Prepare and cut out the terrier pattern pieces.

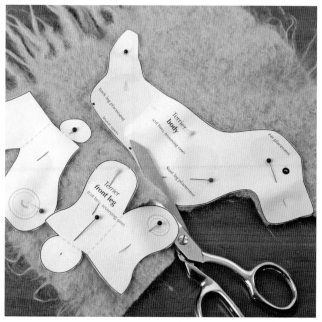

2. Pin the pattern pieces to the wool and cut out, reversing the patterns as indicated, or cut around the freezer paper patterns.

3. Pin the body pieces together with *wrong* sides facing.

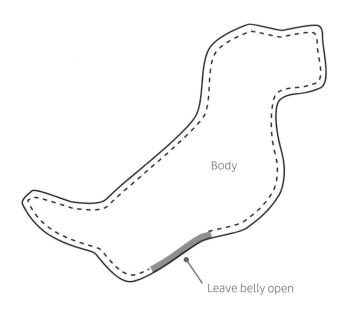

Body

Leave belly open

4. Stitch around the body ⅛" (3.18mm) from the edge, beginning at the belly opening.

Wool roving comes in delightful textures and colors. Have fun finding curls for your terrier.

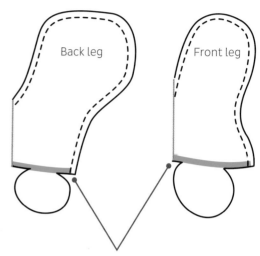

Leave bottom edge of legs open

5. Fill the terrier body firmly with stuffing. Begin with small pieces in the tail. Use a chopstick to push it in and manipulate the shape. Stitch the opening closed.

6. Assemble the legs in the same manner as the Basic Dog. (See steps 11 to 12 on pages 23 to 24.)

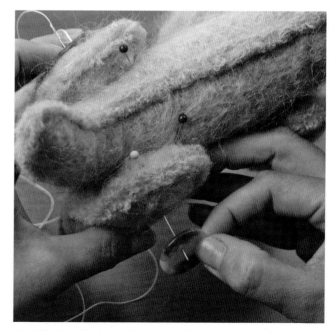

7. Stuff the legs firmly. Fold the foot flap over and stitch it closed.

8. Pin the finished legs to the terrier and sew them in place with buttons.

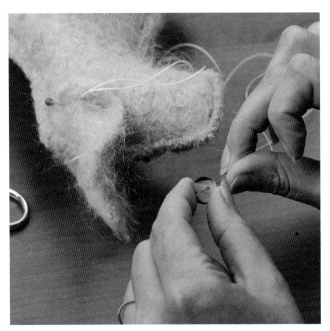

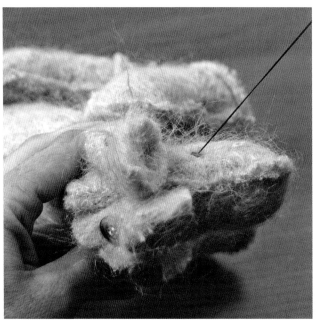

9. Position an ear in place on each side of the head; pin. Using a button on each side, stitch through the head to secure.

10. Sew ¼" (6mm)–diameter buttons in place for eyes. Stitch through the head, pulling the doubled thread to indent the head slightly.

ADDING DETAILS

Adding a beard to the terrier's chin is easy with roving curls and a needle-felting tool. Be careful when working with the tool—it is small and sharp! Don't put your fingers under the terrier's head. The needle-felting tool has barbs that push the roving into the wool. Upholstery foam makes a safe cushion to needle felt on—inexpensive foam remnants can be found at upholstery shops.

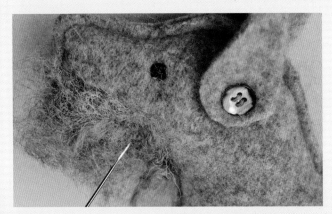

Lay strands of wool roving along the terrier's chin and poke the tool repeatedly into the face. Add pieces a few at a time to build up the beard hair.

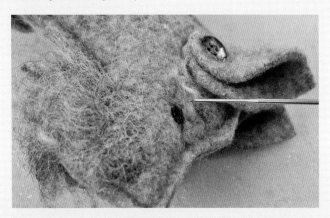

Give the terrier bushy eyebrows with strands of roving.

PATTERNS

*Copy page at 100%

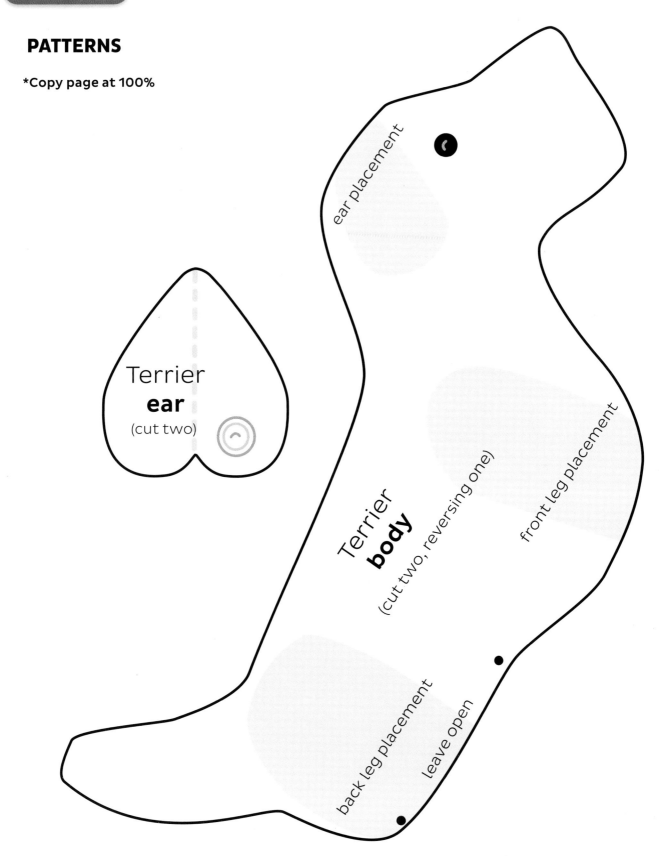

Terrier
ear
(cut two)

ear placement

Terrier
body
(cut two, reversing one)

front leg placement

back leg placement

leave open

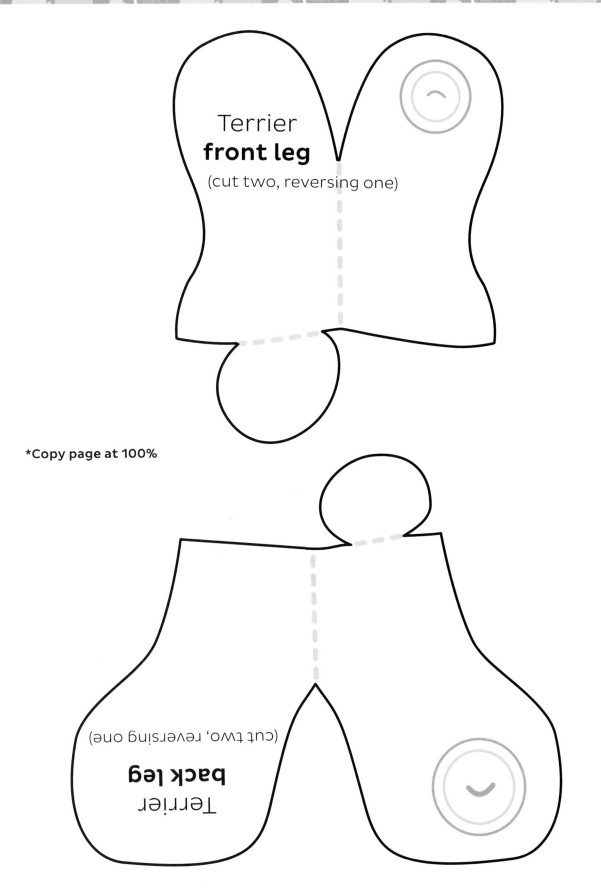

Terrier
front leg
(cut two, reversing one)

*Copy page at 100%

Terrier
back leg
(cut two, reversing one)

CURIOUS CAT

This beautiful cat can be posed to primp, pounce, or prance and even has a tail that can stand straight up when the cat is really interested in something. Go crazy with your color choices to give your project plenty of personality; don't forget about using mohair or plaid!

SUPPLIES

- ¼ yd. (22.86cm) or 9" × 26" (22.8 × 66cm) felted wool fabric
- Buttons:
  - Two 1" to 1¼" (25 to 32mm) buttons, for back legs
  - Two ¾" to 1" (19 to 25mm) buttons, for front legs
  - Two ⅝" to ¾" (16 to 19mm) buttons, for head
  - Two ⅜" (10mm) buttons, for tail
  - Two ⅜" to ½" (10 to 13mm) buttons, for ears
  - Two ¼" (6mm) buttons, for eyes

- Large straight pins
- Large hand-sewing needle
- 5" (127mm) doll (soft sculpture) needle
- Heavy thread or pearl cotton for hand stitching, or sewing thread for machine stitching
- Pearl cotton, for the whiskers
- Wool roving, polyester fiberfill, or wool scraps
- Chopstick or stuffing tool
- Freezer paper (optional)

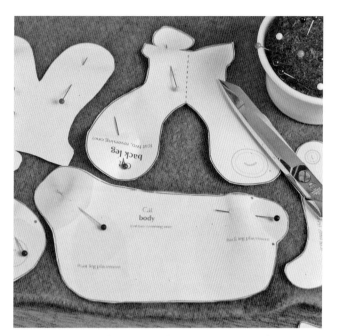

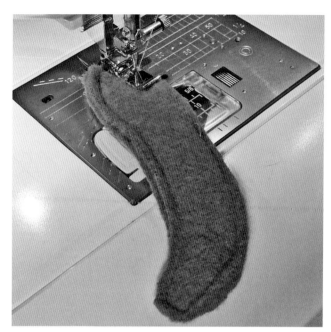

1. Prepare and cut out the cat pattern pieces. Pin the pattern pieces to the wool and cut out, reversing the patterns as indicated, or cut around the freezer paper patterns.

2. Pin the tail pieces together with *wrong* sides facing. Stitch around the tail ⅛" (3.18mm) from the edge; leave an opening for stuffing. See the stitching map for the tail, below.

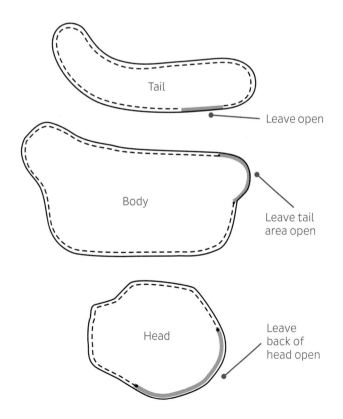

3. Firmly fill the tail with stuffing. Begin with small pieces in the tip. Use a chopstick to push the stuffing in and to manipulate the shape. When it is filled firmly, pin and hand stitch the opening closed.

4. Pin the body pieces together with *wrong* sides facing. Stitch around the body ⅛" (3.18mm) from the edge; leave an opening for stuffing. See the stitching map for the body, opposite.

5. Firmly fill the body with stuffing through the tail opening. Use a chopstick to push the stuffing in and to manipulate the shape.

6. Insert the tail into the body opening and pin it in place. Place a button on either side and sew through all layers. Use a long needle and pearl cotton or doubled heavy thread.

7. Pin the head pieces together with *wrong* sides facing. Stitch around the head ⅛" (3.18mm) from the edge. Leave the neck area open between the dots. See the stitching map for the head, opposite.

8. Fill the nose and the top half of the head with stuffing. Sew ¼" (6mm)–diameter buttons in place for eyes. Stitch through the head, pulling the doubled thread to indent the head slightly. Place the head in position on the body; pin. Add stuffing as needed.

9. To sew the head to the body, put a button on either side and sew through all layers with a doll needle and pearl cotton or doubled heavy thread.

10. Fold each ear with *wrong* sides facing and pin it in place on each side of the head. With a button on each side, stitch through the head to secure the ears. Do not catch the neck in the stitching.

11. Assemble the legs. Fold each leg in half with *wrong* sides facing and pin. Stitch the edges of the leg as far as the foot. See the stitching map for the legs, opposite.

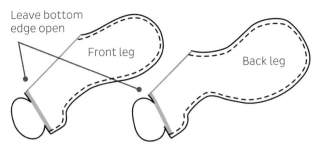

Leave bottom edge open

Front leg

Back leg

12. Stuff the legs firmly. Fold the foot flap over and pin it closed. Hand stitch the toe and side of the foot flap. Add stuffing to shape the foot nicely, then stitch the flap closed.

13. Pin the completed legs in position on the body. Check the position by standing the cat up, and adjust the leg positions as needed.

14. With a button on either side of a pair of legs, sew through all layers with a doll needle and pearl cotton or doubled heavy thread. In the same manner, sew the head to the body.

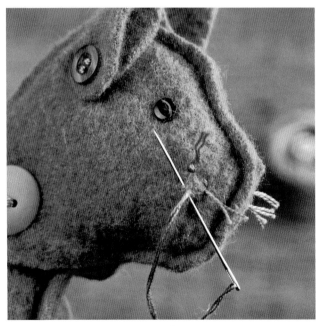

15. Add whiskers by threading pearl cotton or doubled heavy thread on a needle. Take a small stitch and leave a ½" (1.27cm) loose end. Take a second stitch close to the first and pull it tight. Clip to ½" (1.27cm).

PATTERNS

*Copy page at 100%

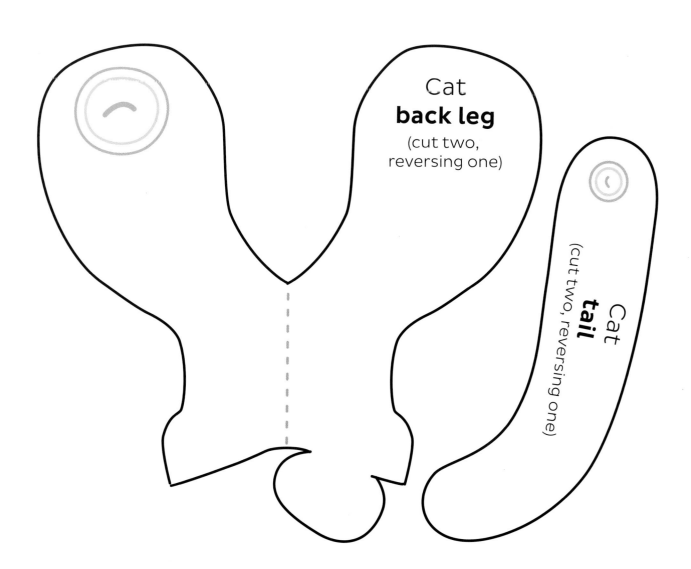

Cat
back leg
(cut two,
reversing one)

Cat
tail
(cut two, reversing one)

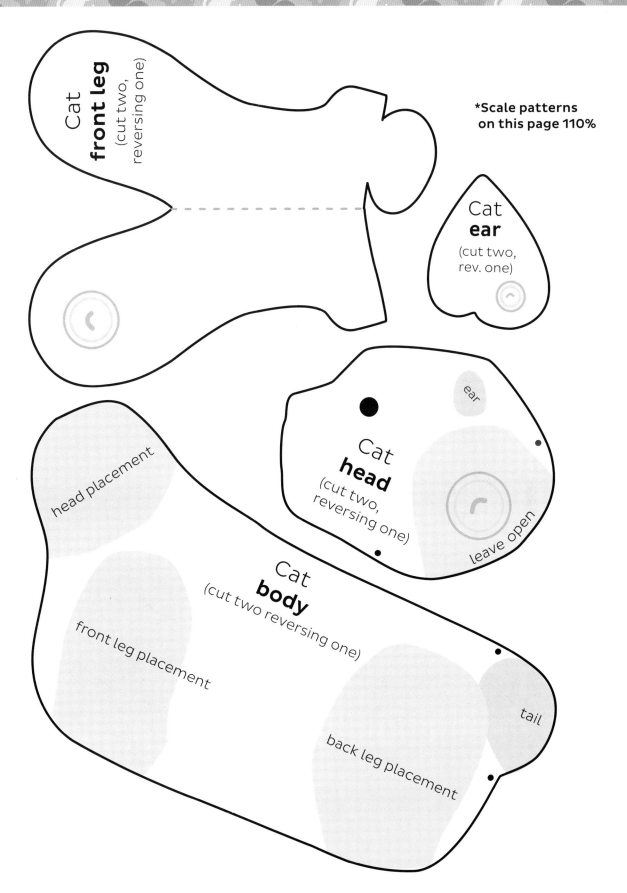

Cat **front leg** (cut two, reversing one)

*Scale patterns on this page 110%

Cat **ear** (cut two, rev. one)

ear

Cat **head** (cut two, reversing one)

leave open

head placement

Cat **body** (cut two reversing one)

front leg placement

back leg placement

tail

MOTHER AND FATHER RABBIT

Nothing says springtime like this cute little rabbit family! Father rabbit, mother rabbit, and bunnies—lots of bunnies—make it clear that spring is in the air. These beautiful rabbits are ideal for adding to Easter baskets, especially when you make them out of felted wool in bright spring colors—even pastel plaids. Adding a pom-pom tail lets you introduce even more color.

SUPPLIES

- ¼ yd. (22.86cm) or 10" × 16" (25.4 × 40.7cm) felted wool fabric
- Buttons:
  - Two 1" to 1¼" (25 to 32mm) buttons, for back legs
  - Two ¾" to 1" (19 to 25mm) buttons, for front legs
  - Two ⅜" to ½" (10 to 13mm) buttons, for ears
  - Two ¼" or ⅜" (6 or 10mm) beads, for eyes
- Large straight pins
- Large hand-sewing needle

- Milliners' or straw needle, for sewing on bead eyes
- 5" to 6" (127 to 152mm) doll (soft sculpture) needle
- Heavy thread for hand stitching, or sewing thread for machine stitching
- Wool roving, polyester fiberfill, or wool scraps
- Yarn and Clover® Pom-Pom Maker, for pom-pom tails (optional)
- Chopstick or stuffing tool
- Freezer paper (optional)

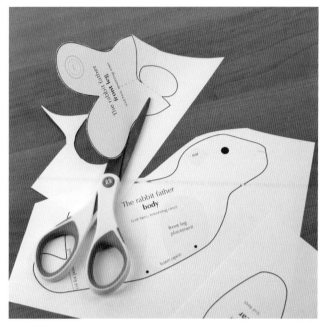

1. Prepare and cut out the rabbit pattern pieces.

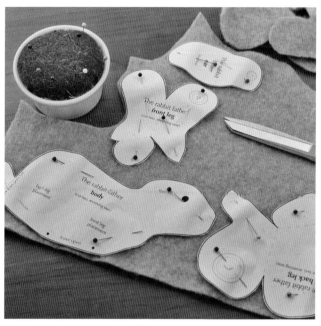

2. Pin the pattern pieces to the wool and cut out, reversing the patterns as indicated, or cut around the freezer paper patterns.

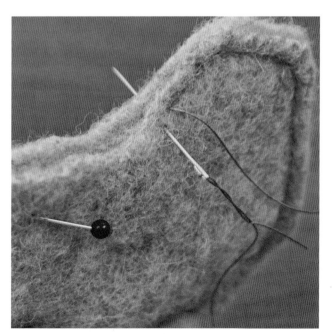

3. Pin the body pieces together with *wrong* sides facing. Stitch around the body ⅛" (3.18mm) from the edge. Leave an opening for stuffing. See the stitching map for the body on the next page.

4. Assemble the legs. Fold each leg in half with *wrong* sides facing and pin. Stitch the edges of the leg as far as the foot. See the stitching map for the legs on the next page.

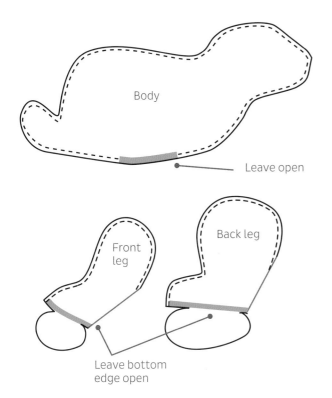

Body

Leave open

Front leg

Back leg

Leave bottom edge open

5. Firmly fill the rabbit body with stuffing. Begin with small pieces in the tail. Use a chopstick to push them in and manipulate the shape. When firm, stitch the opening closed.

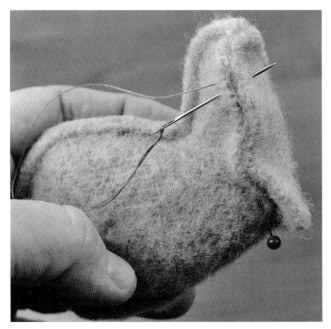

6. Stuff the legs firmly. Fold the foot flap over and pin it closed.

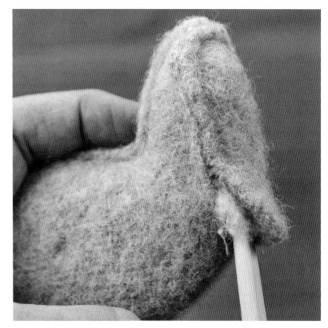

7. Hand stitch the toe and side of the foot flap. Leave the heel open. Add stuffing to shape the foot nicely, then stitch the rest of the flap closed.

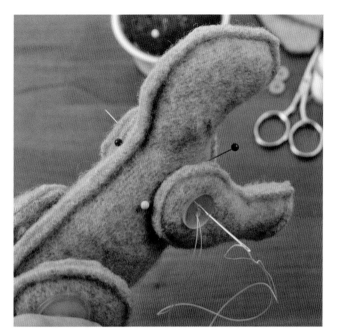

8. Pin the completed legs in position on the rabbit's body. Check the position by standing the rabbit up and adjusting the leg positions as needed. With a button on either side of the legs, sew through all layers with a doll needle and doubled heavy thread.

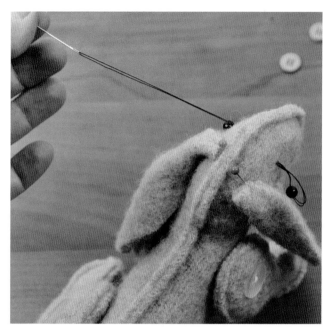

9. Sew ¼" or ⅜" (6 or 10mm)–diameter beads in place for eyes. Use a thin needle that will fit through the beads. Stitch through the head, pulling the doubled thread to indent the head slightly.

10. Fold the ears in half and, referring to the placement markings, pin them in place. Using a button on each side, stitch through the head to secure the ears.

11. Stitch across the nose at the line to shape the nostrils. Use a slightly darker shade of pearl cotton or embroidery floss. End here if you do not wish to add a pom-pom tail to your rabbit.

VARIATION:
Making a Pom-Pom Tail

A variation you may want to try is to use a pom-pom for a rabbit's tail. I used some acrylic yarn and the Clover® Pom-Pom Maker in the 1⅝" (45mm) size to make the father rabbit's tail.

A. Cut off the tail portion of the pattern before making the rabbit's body.

B. Following the manufacturer's directions, wrap yarn around the pom-pom maker's arms.

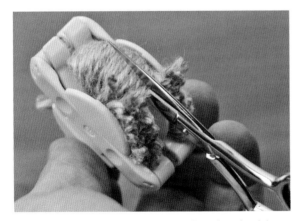

C. After the yarn is wrapped on both sides, close the arms and cut through the center of the yarn with sharp scissors. Wrap heavy thread or yarn around the center and knot securely before removing the pom-pom.

D. Thread one end of the thread or yarn on a needle and use it to sew the pom-pom to the body. Stitch through the body, back through the pom-pom, and repeat. Do the same with the other long end. After knotting the threads securely, trim the ends to match the pom-pom.

PATTERNS

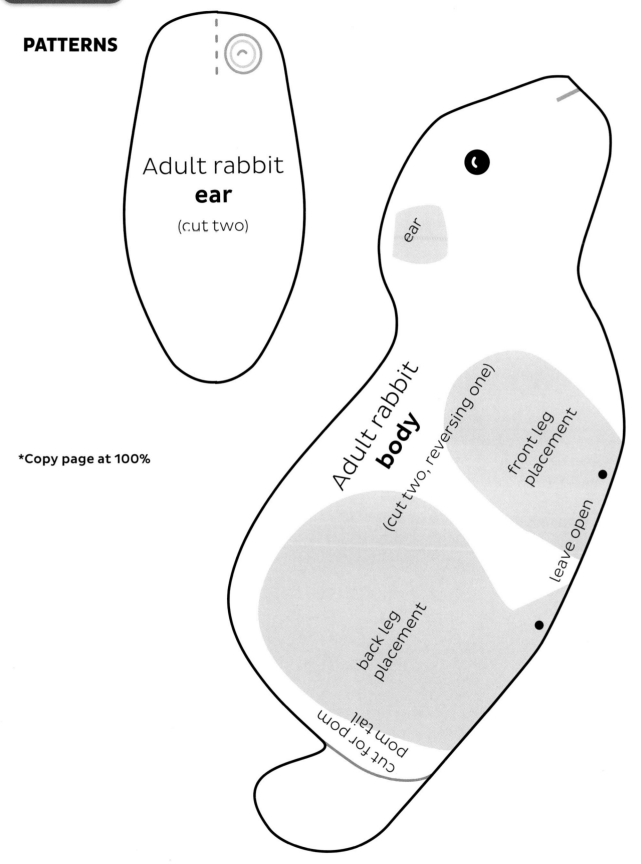

Adult rabbit
ear

(cut two)

*Copy page at 100%

Adult rabbit
body

(cut two, reversing one)

ear

front leg
placement

leave open

back leg
placement

cut for pom
pom tail

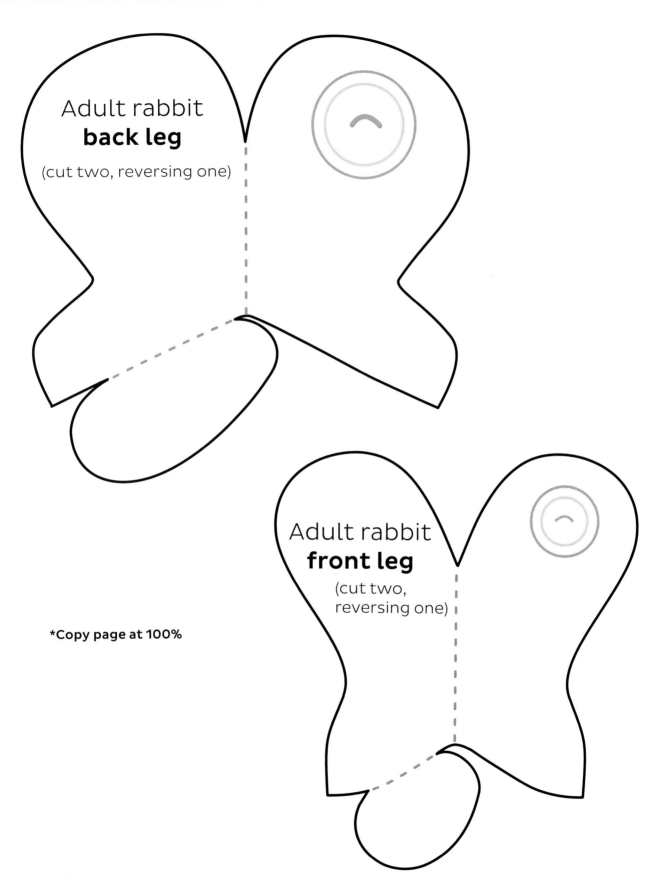

Adult rabbit
back leg
(cut two, reversing one)

Adult rabbit
front leg
(cut two,
reversing one)

*Copy page at 100%

BABY BUNNY

The bunny is made in a very similar fashion as the adult rabbits. Make a bunch of them in different colors to create a large rabbit family.

SUPPLIES

- ¼ yd. (22.86cm) or 9" × 12" (22.8 × 30.5cm) felted wool fabric
- Buttons:
  - Two ⅝" to ¾" (16 to 19mm) buttons, for back legs
  - Two ⅜" (10mm) buttons, for ears
  - Two ¼" or ⅜" (6 or 10mm) beads, for eyes
- Large straight pins
- Large hand-sewing needle
- Milliners' or straw needle, for sewing on bead eyes

- 5" to 6" (127 to 152mm) doll (soft sculpture) needle
- Heavy thread for hand stitching, or sewing thread for machine stitching
- Wool roving, polyester fiberfill, or wool scraps
- Yarn and Clover® Pom-Pom Maker, for pom-pom tails (optional)
- Chopstick or stuffing tool
- Freezer paper (optional)

1. Prepare and cut out the bunny pattern pieces in the same manner as the adult rabbits. Follow steps 1 and 2 on page 46.

2. Pin the body pieces together with *wrong* sides facing. Stitch around the body ⅛" (3.18mm) from the edge, leaving open the area between the dots for the belly insert. See the stitching map for the body, below left.

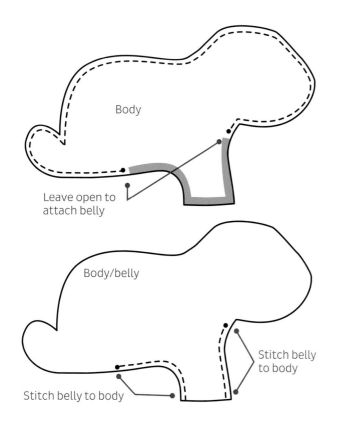

Body

Leave open to attach belly

Body/belly

Stitch belly to body

Stitch belly to body

3. Pin the belly piece in place, matching the legs and the dots. Stitch the belly and the legs as far as the foot. See the stitching map for the body/belly, left.

4. Through the foot openings, fill the bunny with your choice of stuffing. Fold over the foot flaps and pin. Hand stitch the foot flaps in place.

5. Assemble the back legs in the same manner as the adult rabbits. Follow steps 4, 7, and 8 on pages 46 to 48.

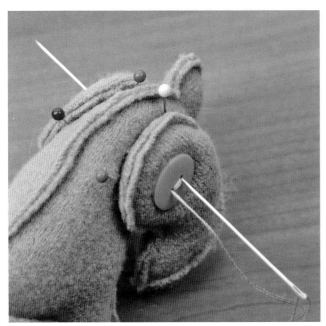

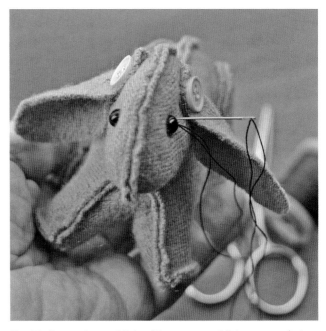

6. Pin the completed back legs to the bunny's body. Check the position by standing the bunny up and adjusting the leg positions as needed. Place a button on either side of the legs and sew through all layers with a doll needle and doubled heavy thread.

7. Follow steps 10 to 11 on page 48 to complete the bunny. Sew on the eyes and ears. Embroider the nose line.

PATTERNS

*Copy page at 100%

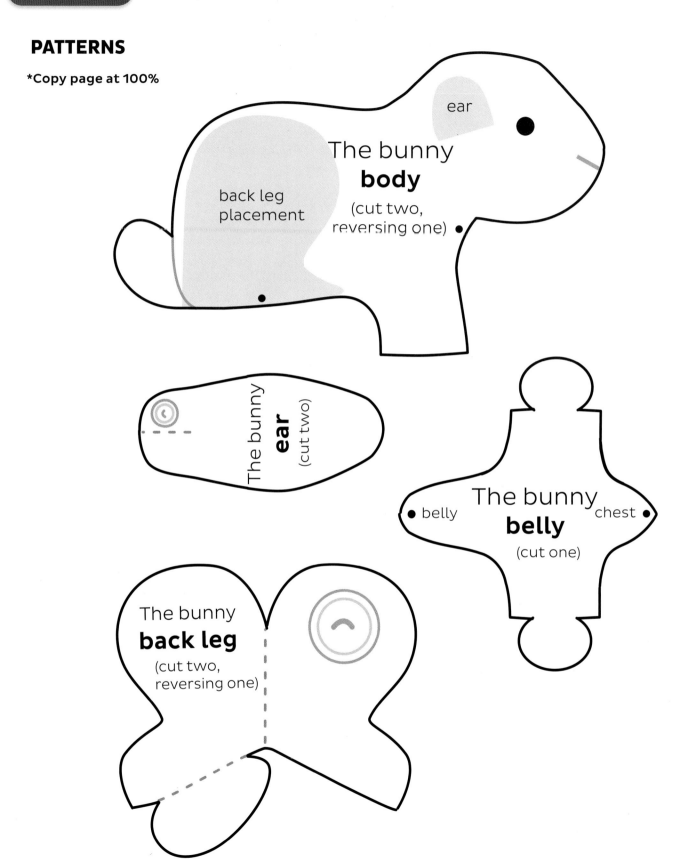

ear

The bunny
body
(cut two,
reversing one)

back leg
placement

The bunny
ear
(cut two)

The bunny
belly
(cut one)

belly

chest

The bunny
back leg
(cut two,
reversing one)

PLUMP HEN

Of all the animals featured in this book, the hen may be the easiest to make. It's a great option if this is your first felted-wool project—great for kids, too! Use thick wool to make the hen, and if the wool has a dappled pattern, all the better. When you are done, you'll have a perky little chicken complete with comb, wattles, and adjustable wings.

SUPPLIES

- Felted wool fabric:
  - ¼ yd. (22.86cm) or 9" × 12" (22.8 × 30.5cm), for body
  - Scrap of red (approximately 2" × 3" [5 × 7.6cm]), for wattle/comb
- Two ½" (13mm) buttons, for wings
- Two black E-beads or black embroidery floss or pearl cotton, for eyes
- Pearl cotton or embroidery floss, to embroider beak
- To add weight, choose one of these: heavy washer, fishing weight, or ½ cup (95g) of plastic pellets or dried beans

- Large straight pins
- Large hand-sewing needle
- Milliners' or straw needle, for sewing on bead eyes
- Heavy thread or pearl cotton for hand stitching, or sewing thread for machine stitching
- Wool roving, polyester fiberfill, or wool scraps
- Chopstick or stuffing tool
- Ultrafine marker
- Freezer paper (optional)

CHOOSE THE RIGHT WEIGHT OF WOOL FOR YOUR PROJECT

Wool felts into many different thicknesses (see page 6). A felted sweater will result in thicker fabric than wool felted from a thin wool garment. Some animals will work with either thick or thin wool. However, the hen needs to be made of thick wool because the tail needs to stand on its own. If a specific weight is needed for projects in this book, the instructions will include that information.

A good thickness to use for the hen

Too thin to use for the hen

1. Prepare and cut out the hen pattern pieces. Pin the patterns to a single layer of wool and cut out carefully, or cut around the freezer paper patterns.

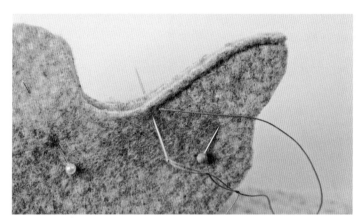

2. Pin the head and back together with *wrong* sides facing. Beginning at the tip of the tail and stitching ⅛" (3.18mm) from the raw edge, join the top edge of the body to the head.

3. Pin the comb in place between the head pieces. Stitch across the head, catching the comb in the stitches. Stitch the beak and chest to the dot.

GIVE THE HEN SOME WEIGHT

It's helpful to weigh the hen down so she will sit nicely. Here are a couple of options:

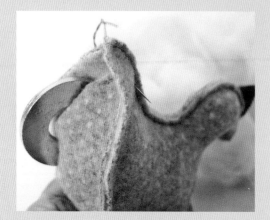

Put a heavy washer through the opening and rotate it to lie at the bottom of the hen. Continue stuffing her firmly and stitch the opening closed.

Or you can pour ½ cup (95g) of dried beans or plastic pellets into the hen's belly. Continue stuffing her firmly and stitch the opening closed.

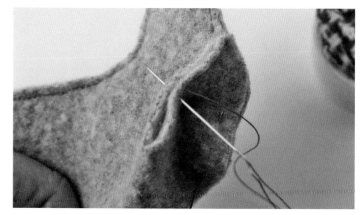

4. Pin the front chest triangle to the body; stitch each side, using a ⅛" (3.18mm) seam allowance.

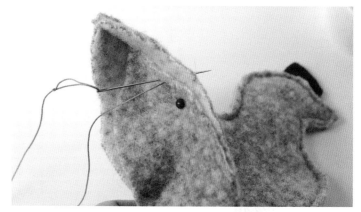

5. Fold up the back flap along the shaded line. Pin in place. Stitch, leaving an opening on one side for stuffing.

6. Firmly stuff the top half of the hen, beginning with small pieces to fill the head. Use a chopstick to manipulate the shape.

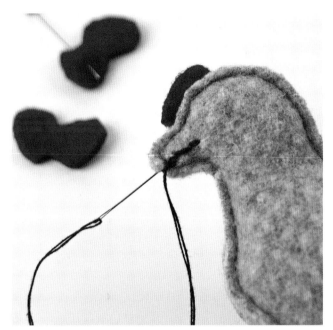

7. Embroider the beak with pearl cotton or embroidery floss. As a guide, lightly mark the beak first with an ultrafine marker.

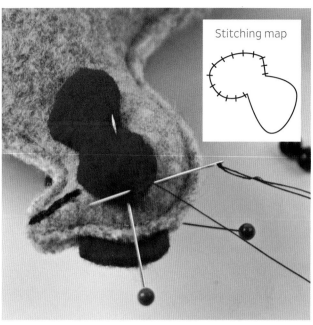

Stitching map

8. Position a wattle on each side of the head, and pin. Using thread to match the wattle, stitch around the top section of each. Leave the bottom half loose.

9. Sew ¼" or ⅜" (6 or 10mm)–diameter beads in place for eyes. Use a thin needle that will fit through the beads. Stitch through the head, pulling the doubled thread to indent the head slightly. Or embroider eyes with black embroidery floss or pearl cotton.

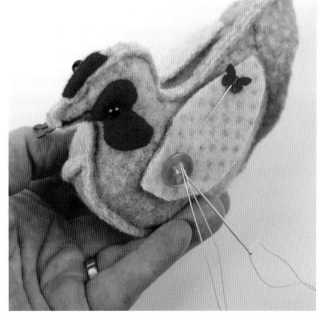

10. If desired, position a wing on each side of the body, and pin. Hold a button on each wing. Using a doubled strand of heavy thread in a doll needle, stitch through the body to secure.

PATTERNS

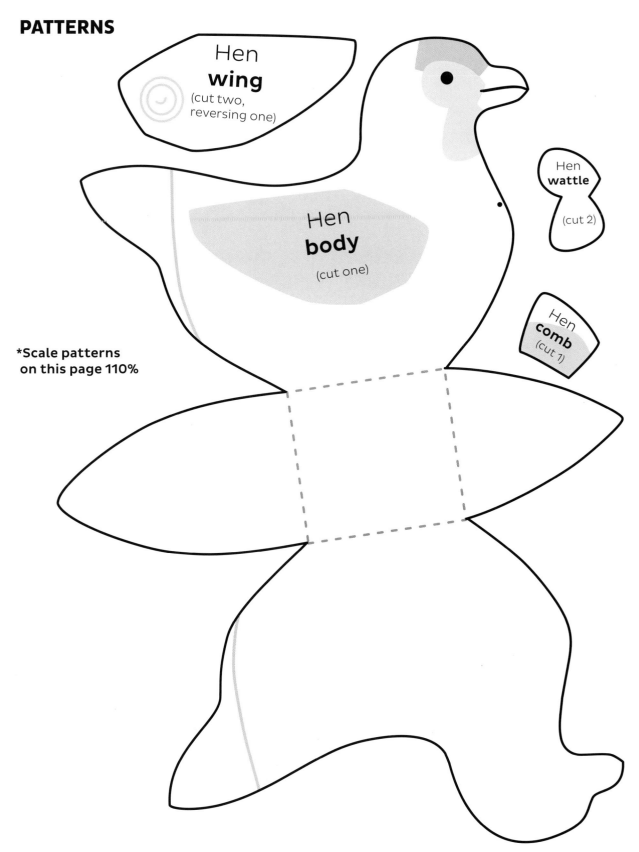

Hen **wing**
(cut two, reversing one)

Hen **body**
(cut one)

Hen **wattle**
(cut 2)

Hen **comb**
(cut 1)

*Scale patterns on this page 110%

Delightful Duck

Looking like it is gently paddling across a barnyard pond, this duck is a great example of how a straight piece (the belly) can join with curved pieces (the sides) to make a 3D, rounded shape. You can opt to attach the wings with buttons. Use buttons or beads for the eyes or, for an infant-safe option, embroider them. All in all, the duck goes together much like the chicken.

SUPPLIES

- Felted wool fabric:
  - ¼ yd. (22.86cm) or 12" × 14" (30.5 × 35.6cm), for body
  - 2" × 4" (5 × 10.16cm), for bill
- Two ½" to ¾" (13 to 19mm) buttons, for wings
- Two black E-beads or black embroidery floss or pearl cotton, for eyes
- To add weight, choose one of these: heavy washer, fishing weight, or ½ cup (95g) of plastic pellets or dried beans
- Large straight pins
- Large hand-sewing needle
- Milliners' or straw needle, for sewing on bead eyes
- Heavy thread or pearl cotton for hand stitching, or sewing thread for machine stitching
- Wool roving, polyester fiberfill, or wool scraps
- Chopstick or stuffing tool
- Fine-tip marker
- Freezer paper (optional)

MARKING ON WOOL

It is helpful to mark the belly and body pieces so you can pin them together accurately. Wool can be difficult to mark. Here are a couple of ideas for how to do it.

On the wrong side of the fabric, mark with a fine-tip marker.

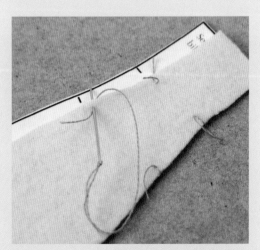

Or make a small stitch at each mark, using a contrasting color thread. Do not knot. Pull out the marking threads after stitching.

1. Prepare and cut out the duck pattern pieces. Pin the patterns to a single layer of wool and cut out carefully, or cut around the freezer paper patterns.

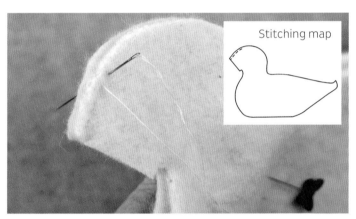

Stitching map

2. Pin the body pieces together with *wrong* sides facing. Stitching ⅛" (3.18mm) from the raw edge, join the top edge of the body from the bill for about 1½" (3.8cm).

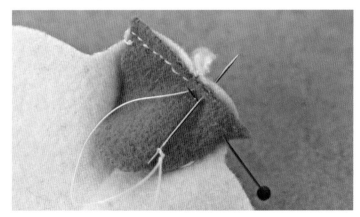

3. Open the straight edge of the head and pin the upper bill piece to it with *wrong* sides facing. Stitching ⅛" (3.18mm) from the raw edge, join the upper bill to the body.

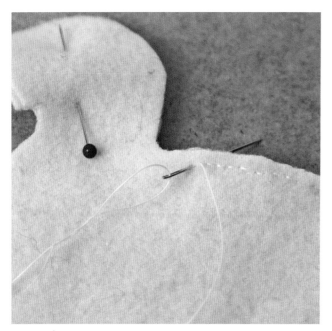

4. Pin the body pieces back together and continue sewing the body from the tip of the tail to the bill.

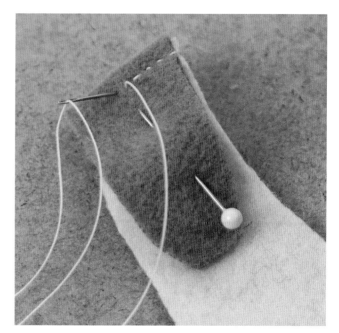

5. Pin the lower bill piece to the straight edge of the belly with *wrong* sides facing. Stitching ⅛" (3.18mm) from the raw edge, join the lower bill to the belly.

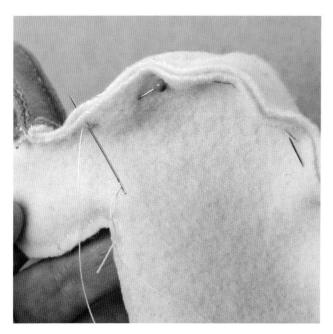

6. Working on one side at a time, match the markings on the body and the belly. Sew from the tip of the bill to the tail on each side. Leave an opening on one side for stuffing.

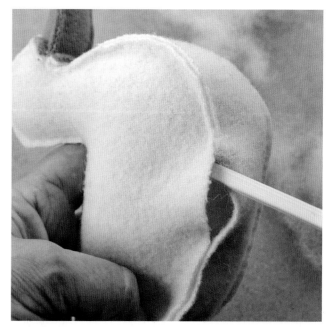

7. Fill the duck firmly with the stuffing of your choice. Begin with small pieces in the bill and the head. Use a chopstick to push it in and manipulate the shape.

8. Put some weight (like a heavy washer) in the bottom of the duck. (See tip on page 60.) Finish stuffing her firmly. Stitch the opening closed.

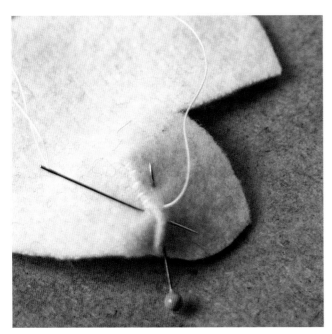

9. If you want wings, overlap the clip of each and stitch it closed. If your fabric is thick, clip out the overlay and stitch the edges together instead of overlapping them. Or if you have very thick wool, cut wings from a single layer of wool.

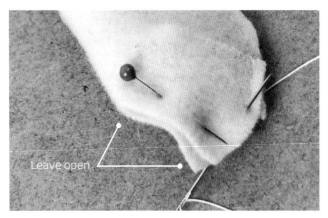

Leave open

10. Fold the wing with *wrong* sides facing and stitch around the outside edge. Add a small amount of stuffing before stitching each wing closed.

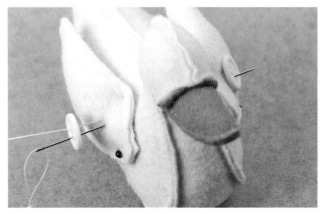

11. Position a wing on each side of the body, and pin. Hold a button on either side. Using a doubled strand of heavy thread in a doll needle, stitch through the body to secure.

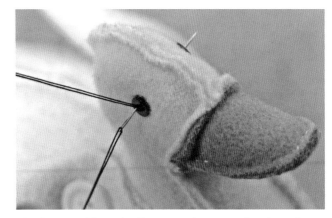

12. Sew ¼" (6mm)–diameter buttons in place for eyes. Stitch through the head, pulling the doubled thread to indent the head slightly.

PATTERNS

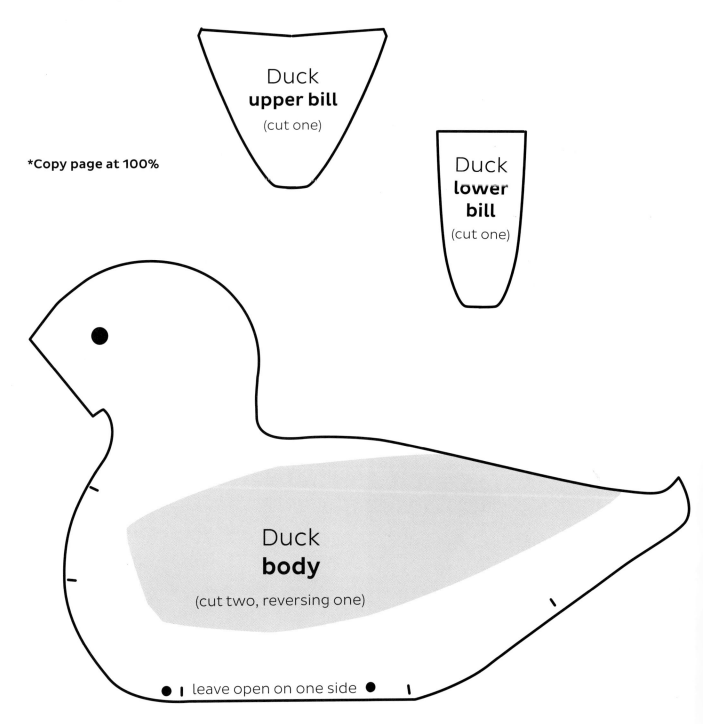

Duck
upper bill
(cut one)

Duck
lower bill
(cut one)

*Copy page at 100%

Duck
body
(cut two, reversing one)

leave open on one side

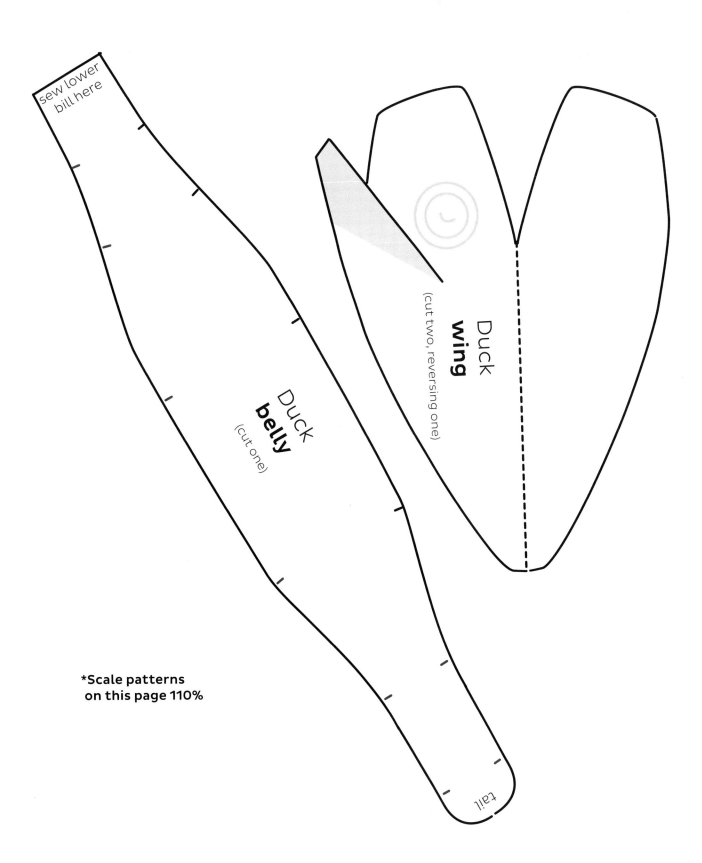

sew lower
bill here

Duck
belly
(cut one)

Duck
wing
(cut two, reversing one)

tail

***Scale patterns
on this page 110%**

LITTLE DUCKLING

Go traditional or get creative with the wool colors and patterns you choose for your ducklings. I chose to use a fun patterned brown fabric for one and a soft yellow for the other. Don't forget that you can customize the duckling's bill, like I did here with the yellow duckling's blue bill.

SUPPLIES

- Felted wool fabric:
  - ⅛ yd. (11.43 cm) or 8" × 10" (20.3 × 25.4cm), for body
  - 2" × 3" (5 × 7.6cm), for bill
- Two ½" to ¾" (13 to 19mm) buttons, for wings
- Two black E-beads or black embroidery floss or pearl cotton, for eyes
- To add weight, choose one of these: heavy washer, fishing weight, or ½ cup (95g) of plastic pellets or dried beans
- Large straight pins
- Large hand-sewing needle
- Milliners' or straw needle, for sewing on bead eyes
- Heavy thread or pearl cotton for hand stitching, or sewing thread for machine stitching
- Wool roving, polyester fiberfill, or wool scraps
- Chopstick or stuffing tool
- Freezer paper (optional)

1. The duckling is made in the same manner as the adult duck (page 64). The only difference is that the bill is one piece for the duckling, so skip over step 3 from the adult duck project. Sew the upper bill to the straight edge of the head and the lower bill to the body. Continue assembling the duckling in the same way as you assembled the duck.

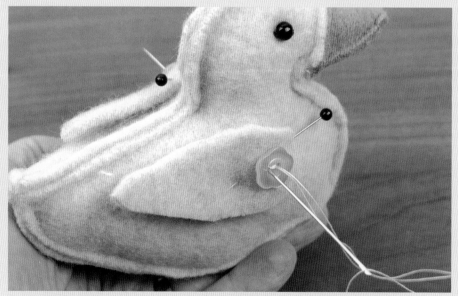

2. Cut the optional duckling wings from a single layer of wool. Pin one on each side of the body. Place a button on either side, and using a doubled strand of heavy thread in a doll needle, stitch through the body to secure.

PATTERNS

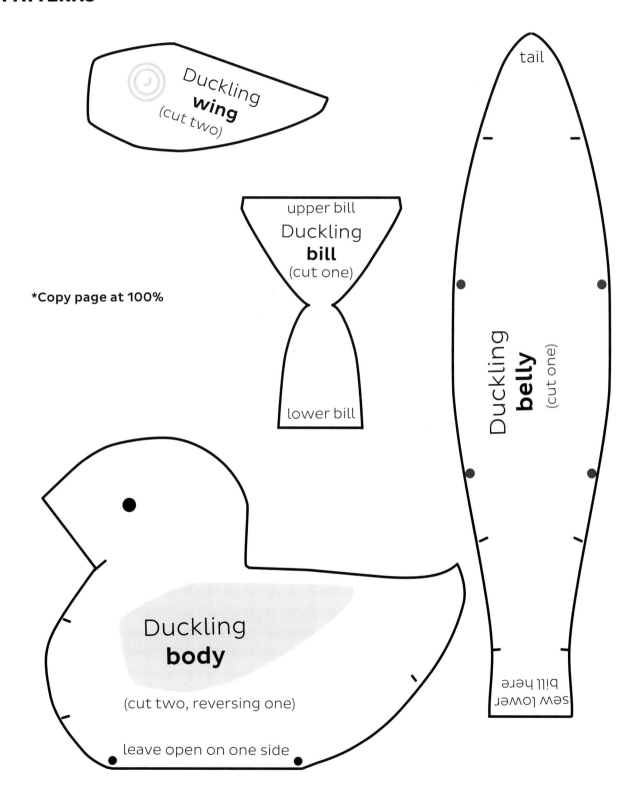

Duckling **wing** (cut two)

upper bill
Duckling **bill**
(cut one)

lower bill

*Copy page at 100%

tail

Duckling **belly** (cut one)

sew lower bill here

Duckling **body**

(cut two, reversing one)

leave open on one side

PORTLY
PIG

From its curled tail to the tip of its inquisitive nose, this smart little pig is ready to take on the world. Pink is a natural color for the pig, but remember that pigs can be white, black, rust, brown, and gray—with spots and stripes, too! And because pig ears are cupped, you'll fold your pig's ears before attaching them.

SUPPLIES

- ⅓ yd. (30.48cm) or 12" × 24" (30.5 × 61cm) felted wool fabric
- Buttons:
  - Two 1" to 1¼" (25 to 32mm) buttons, for back legs
  - Two ¾" (19mm) buttons, for front legs
  - Two ½" to ¾" (13 to 19mm) buttons, for head
  - Two ¼" to ⅜" (6 to 10mm) buttons, for ears
  - Two ¼" (6mm) buttons, for eyes
- Large straight pins

- Large hand-sewing needle
- 5" (127mm) doll (soft sculpture) needle
- Quilting or buttonhole thread for hand stitching, or sewing thread for machine stitching
- Pearl cotton or embroidery floss, for embroidering features
- Wool roving, polyester fiberfill, or wool scraps
- Chopstick or stuffing tool
- Freezer paper (optional)

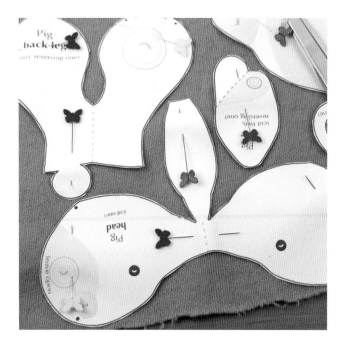

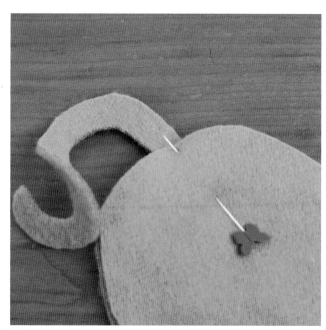

1. Prepare and cut out the pig pattern pieces. Pin the pattern pieces to the wool and cut out, reversing the patterns as indicated, or cut around the freezer paper patterns.

2. Pin the body pieces together with *wrong* sides facing, with the tail in place at the mark. Stitch around the body ⅛" (3.18mm) from the edge; leave an opening for stuffing. See the stitching map for the body, below left.

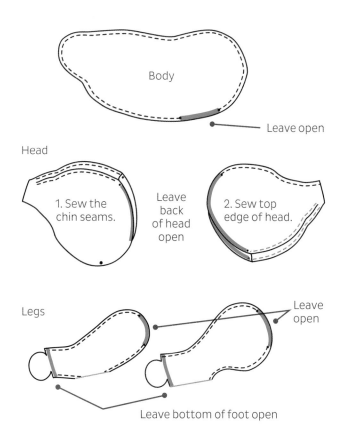

Body

Leave open

Head

1. Sew the chin seams.

Leave back of head open

2. Sew top edge of head.

Legs

Leave open

Leave bottom of foot open

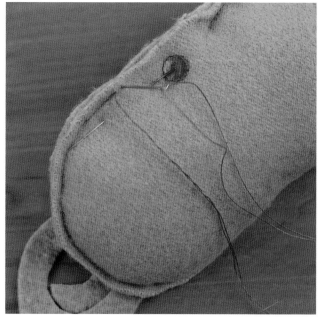

3. Firmly fill the body with stuffing. Use a chopstick to push the stuffing in and to manipulate the shape. When the body is filled firmly, pin and hand stitch the opening closed.

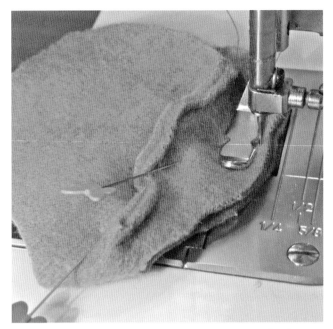

Leave open

4. Fold the chin piece with *wrong* sides facing to match one lower edge of the head, pinning it to one side; stitch from the dot to the nose. Then repeat to sew the other side. See the stitching map for the head, below opposite.

5. Fold the head at the nose with *wrong* sides facing; stitch the top of the head from the dot to the nose. Leave the neck area open between the dots.

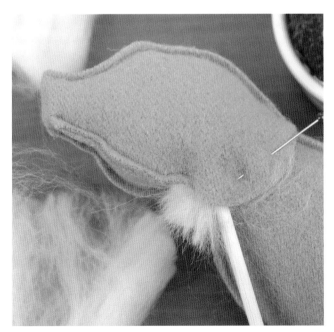

6. Fill the front half of the head with stuffing. Place the head in position on the body; pin. Add stuffing as needed to give the head a pleasing shape.

7. Assemble the legs. Fold each leg in half with *wrong* sides facing and pin. Stitch the edges of the leg as far as the foot. See the stitching map for the legs, opposite.

OPTIONAL: STRENGTHEN THE LEGS

If you feel that your wool and stuffing aren't sturdy enough to enable your animal to stand by itself, you can strengthen the legs by inserting something inside to stiffen them. Use either vinyl-coated mesh (also called pet screen), which is made from PVC and polyester, or use an interfacing like a heavyweight stabilizer such as Pellon® 71F Peltex®. Fuse the Peltex to a piece of wool before rolling it into a tube.

Leave an opening at the top of each leg as well as the bottom to make it easier to stuff around the stiffener.

A. To stiffen the legs with vinyl-coated mesh, cut four 3" × 5" (7.6 x 12.7cm) pieces for the pig. Roll the mesh from the short end.

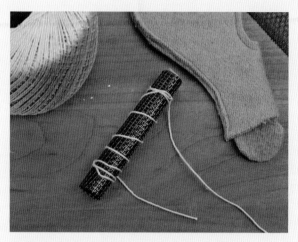

B. Wrap the mesh with pearl cotton or heavy thread, and knot each end to secure the roll.

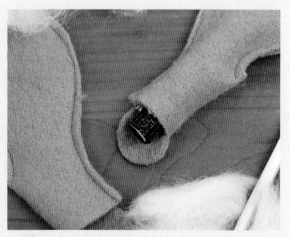

C. Slide a mesh roll into the bottom end of each leg. Then stuff the bottom of the leg firmly around the roll with your choice of stuffing. Fold the foot flap over and pin it closed.

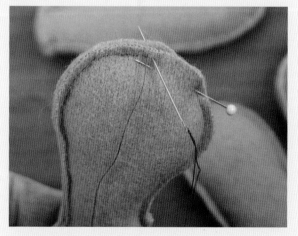

D. Hand stitch the foot flap. Finish stuffing the legs firmly from the top opening. Hand stitch the top opening closed.

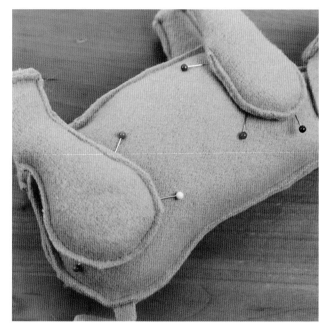

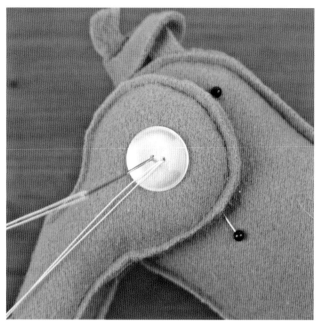

8. Pin the completed legs in position on the body. Check the position by standing the pig up and adjusting the leg positions as needed.

9. Place a button on either side of a pair of legs. Sew through all layers with a doll needle and pearl cotton or doubled heavy thread. In the same manner, sew the head to the body.

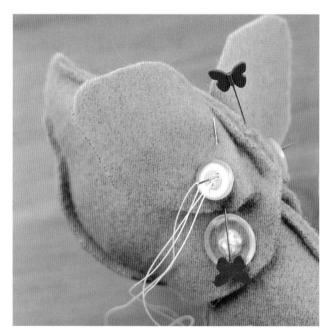

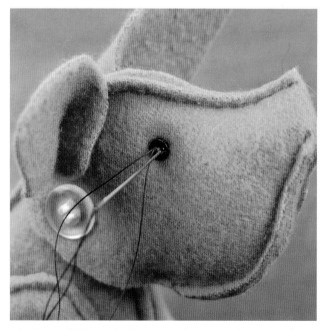

10. Following the pattern marking, fold each ear with *wrong* sides facing and pin it in place on the head. With a button on each side, stitch through the head to secure the ears. Do not catch the neck in the stitching.

11. Sew ¼" (6mm)–diameter buttons in place for eyes. Stitch through the head, pulling the doubled thread to indent the head slightly.

PATTERNS

*Scale patterns
on this page 110%

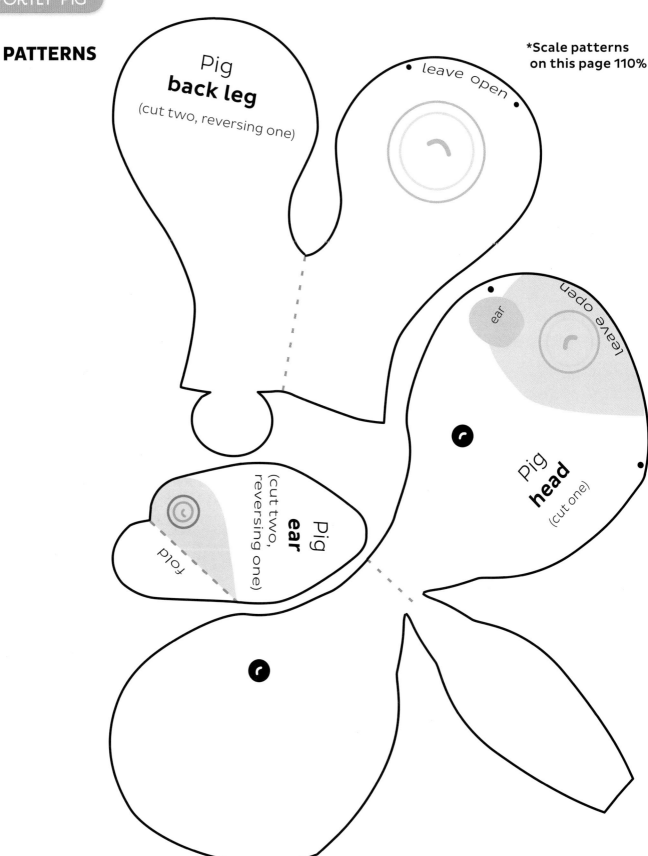

Pig
back leg
(cut two, reversing one)

leave open

Pig
head
(cut one)

leave open

ear

Pig
ear
(cut two,
reversing one)

Fold

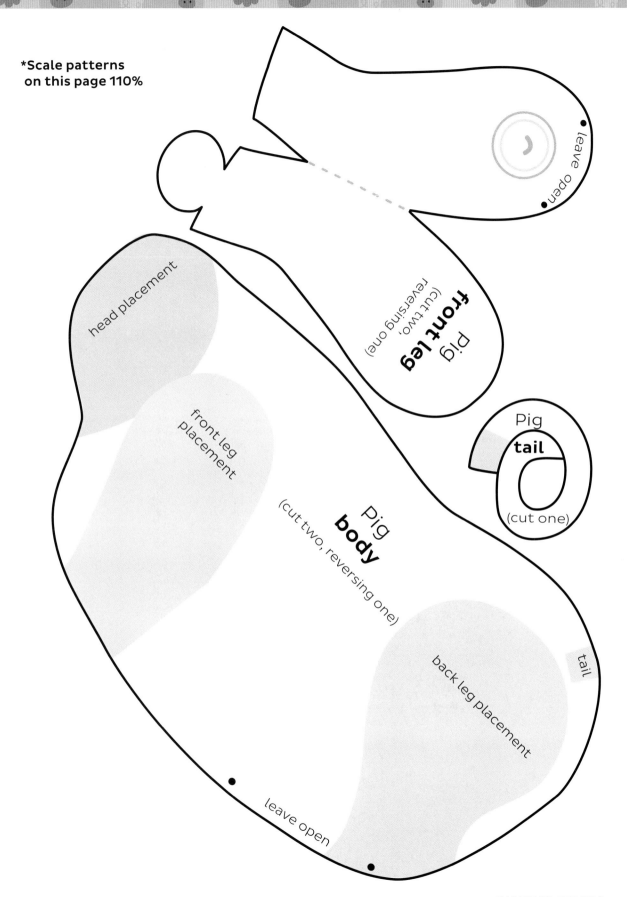

*Scale patterns on this page 110%

leave open

Pig
front leg
(cut two, reversing one)

head placement

front leg placement

Pig
body
(cut two, reversing one)

Pig
tail
(cut one)

back leg placement

tail

leave open

SPIRITED PONY

With a yarn mane, tail, and even an optional blaze of color on its head, this project is a great answer for that birthday wish of every child—a pony! To capture every horsey emotion, the ears are posable. This project is slightly more complex than some but still easily completed in a few hours.

SUPPLIES

- ⅓ yd. (30.48cm) or 12" × 36" (30.5 × 91.4cm) felted wool fabric
- Buttons:
  - Four 1" to 1¼" (25 to 32mm) buttons, for legs
  - Two ⅝" to ¾" (16 to 19mm) buttons, for head
  - Two ⅜" to ½" (10 to 13mm) buttons, for ears
  - Two ⅜" (10mm) buttons, for eyes
- Large straight pins
- Large hand-sewing needle
- 5" (127mm) doll (soft sculpture) needle

- Heavy thread or pearl cotton for hand stitching, or sewing thread for machine stitching
- Black pearl cotton or embroidery floss, for features
- Yarn, for mane
- Wool roving, polyester fiberfill, or wool scraps
- Chopstick or stuffing tool
- Permanent marker
- Freezer paper (optional)

1. Prepare and cut out the pony pattern pieces. Pin the pattern pieces to the wool and cut out, reversing the patterns as indicated, or cut around the freezer paper patterns.

2. Appliqué the blaze to the center of the pony's head if desired. Use thread to match the blaze.

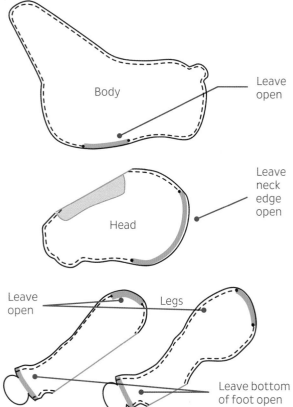

Body

Leave open

Leave neck edge open

Head

Leave open

Legs

Leave bottom of foot open

3. Pin the head together with *wrong* sides facing and stitch ⅛" (3.18mm) from the edge. Refer to the stitching map for the head, left. Leave the neck area open between the dots.

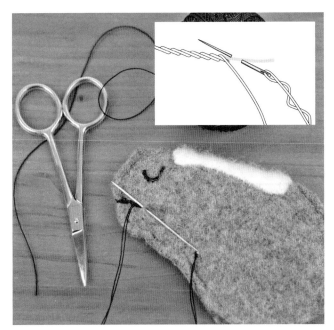

4. Embroider the nose and mouth, using black pearl cotton or embroidery floss. Lightly mark the features with a permanent marker. Work a stem stitch (inset).

5. Pin the body together with *wrong* sides facing. Stitch around the body ⅛" (3.18mm) from the edge, beginning at the belly opening. Leave an opening for stuffing. See the stitching map for the body, opposite below.

6. Firmly fill the body with stuffing. Work with small pieces. Use a chopstick to push them in and manipulate the shape. When firm, hand stitch the opening closed.

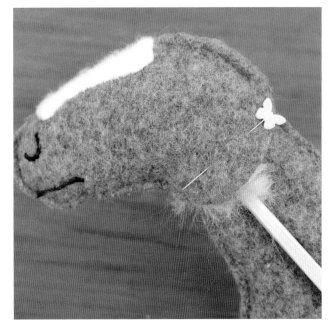

7. Fill the front half of the head with stuffing. Place the head in position on the neck, and pin. Add stuffing as needed to give the head a pleasing shape. Place a button on either side and sew through all layers with a doll needle and doubled heavy thread.

8. Thread a long piece of yarn, at least 32" (81.3cm), on a large-eye needle. Stitch through the neck, pulling the doubled yarn to leave a 3" (7.6cm) loose end. Take a second stitch close to the first.

9. Pull the yarn snug against the body. Leave the next stitch loose (3" [7.6cm] length). Continue, pulling the yarn tight between each loose stitch to lock the loops. Repeat until you have a full mane.

10. Stitch the tail in the same manner, with long doubled pieces of yarn. Stitch through the tail stub, leaving the yarn in about 5½" (14cm)–long strands. Pull the yarn tight between each loose stitch.

11. Fold each ear and pin it in place on the head. Stitch through the head with a button on each side to secure the ears. Sew buttons in place for eyes, pulling the doubled thread to indent the head slightly.

12. Assemble the legs by folding each in half with *wrong* sides facing and pin. Stitch ⅛" (3.18mm) from the edges of the leg. See the stitching map for the legs, page 84.

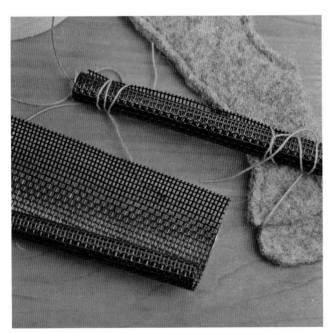

13. As described on page 78, a method of stiffening the legs is to use vinyl-coated mesh or an interfacing such as Pellon® 71F Peltex®. Cut four 4½" by 4½" (11.43 x 11.43cm) pieces. Roll up the mesh into a tube. Wrap it with pearl cotton or heavy thread, and knot each end to secure the roll.

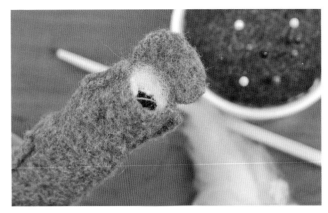

14. Slide a mesh roll into the bottom end of each leg. Then stuff the bottom of the leg firmly around the roll with your choice of stuffing. Fold the foot flap over, and pin it closed.

15. Hand stitch the foot flap. Finish stuffing each leg firmly from the top opening. Hand stitch the top opening closed.

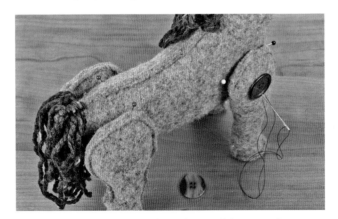

16. Pin the completed legs in position on the pony's body. Check the position by standing the pony up and adjusting the leg positions as needed. With a button on either side of the legs, sew through all layers with a doll needle and doubled heavy thread.

PATTERNS

*Copy page at 100%

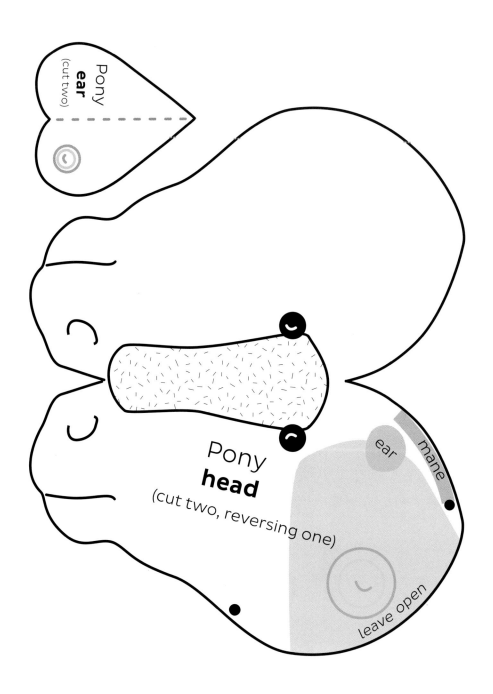

Pony
ear
(cut two)

Pony
head
(cut two, reversing one)

ear

mane

leave open

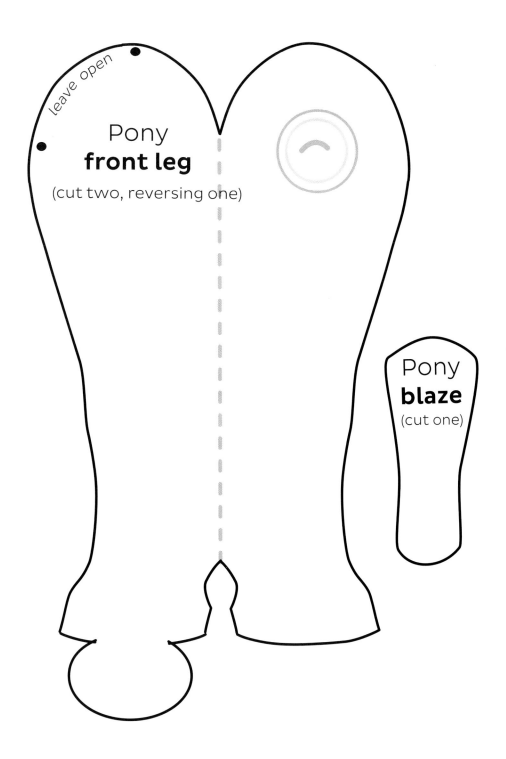

Pony
front leg
(cut two, reversing one)

leave open

Pony
blaze
(cut one)

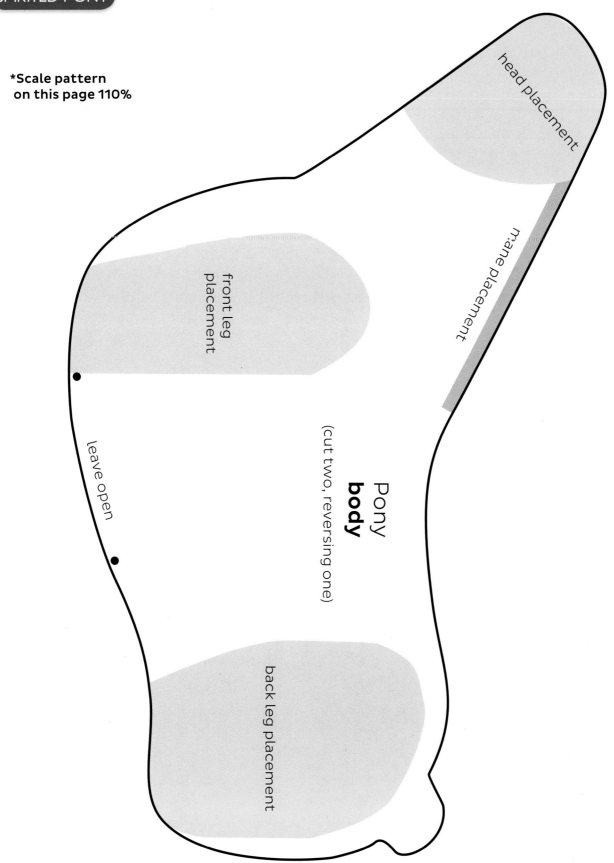

*Scale pattern on this page 110%

head placement

mane placement

front leg placement

leave open

Pony
body
(cut two, reversing one)

back leg placement

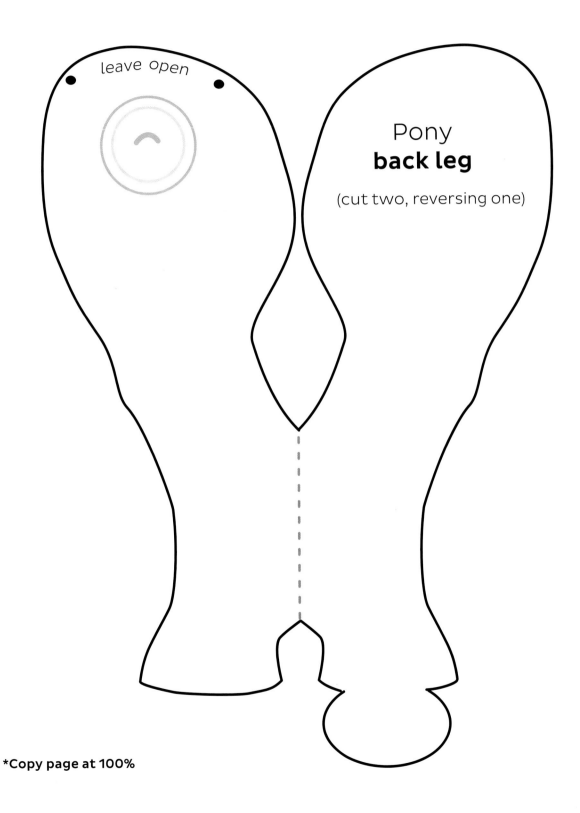

leave open

Pony
back leg

(cut two, reversing one)

*Copy page at 100%

MEADOW GOAT

If you've ever been around goats, you know that they are curious, social, and full of mischief. This goat's posable head tips up for browsing—a goat's favorite activity. Big ears and a perky tail give this project plenty of personality.

SUPPLIES

- ⅓ yd. (30.48cm) or 12" × 24" (30.5 × 61cm) felted wool fabric
- Buttons:
  - Two 1" to 1¼" (25 to 32mm) buttons, for back legs
  - Two ¾" to 1" (19 to 25mm) buttons, for front legs
  - Two ⅝" to ¾" (16 to 19mm) buttons, for head
  - Two ⅜" to ½" (10 to 13mm) buttons, for ears
  - Two ¼" (6mm) buttons, for eyes
- Large straight pins
- Large hand-sewing needle
- 5" (127mm) doll (soft sculpture) needle
- Heavy thread or pearl cotton for hand stitching, or sewing thread for machine stitching
- Pearl cotton or embroidery floss, for embroidering features
- Wool roving, polyester fiberfill, or wool scraps
- Chopstick or stuffing tool
- Permanent marker
- Freezer paper (optional)

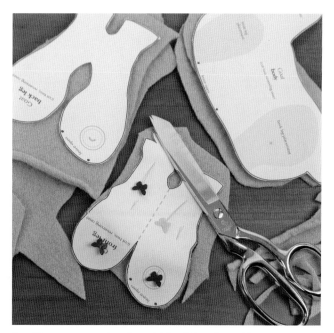

1. Prepare and cut out the Meadow Goat pattern pieces.

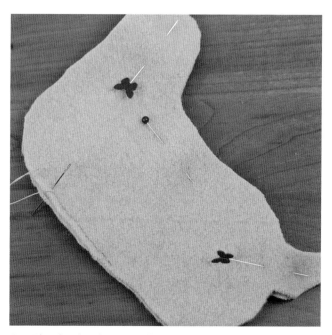

2. Pin the body together with *wrong* sides facing. Stitch around the body ⅛" (3.18mm) from the edge, beginning at the belly opening. Leave an opening for stuffing. See the stitching map for the body, below.

Body

Leave open

Head

Leave neck edge open

Legs

Leave bottom edge open

3. Firmly fill the body with stuffing. Begin by putting small pieces in the tail. Use a chopstick to push them in and manipulate the shape. When firm, hand stitch the opening closed.

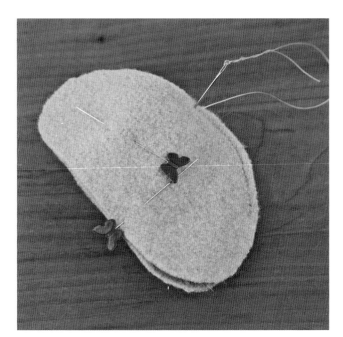

4. Pin the head pieces together with *wrong* sides facing and stitch around the head ⅛" (3.18mm) from the edge. Leave the neck area open between the dots.

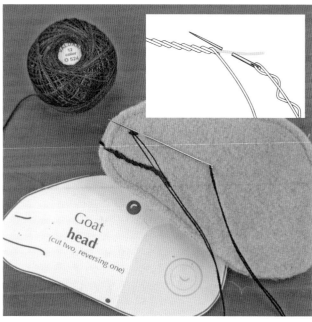

5. Embroider the nose and mouth, using black pearl cotton or embroidery floss. Lightly mark the features with a permanent marker. Work a stem stitch (inset).

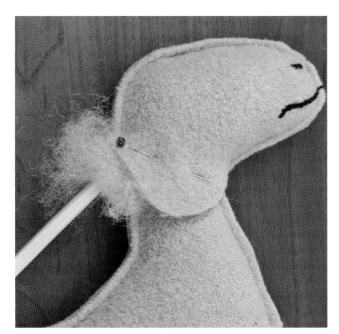

6. Fill the front half of the head with stuffing. Place the head in position on the body; pin. Add stuffing as needed to give the head a pleasing shape. Place a button on either side and sew through all layers with a doll needle and doubled heavy thread.

7. Fold each ear with *wrong* sides facing and pin it in place on each side of the head. With a button on each side, stitch through the head to secure the ears. Be careful not to catch the neck in the stitching.

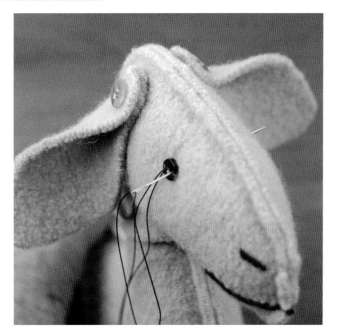

8. Sew ¼" (6mm)–diameter buttons in place for eyes. Stitch through the head, pulling the doubled thread to indent the head slightly.

9. Assemble the legs. Fold each leg in half with *wrong* sides facing and pin. Stitch the edges of the leg as far as the foot. See the stitching map for the legs, below.

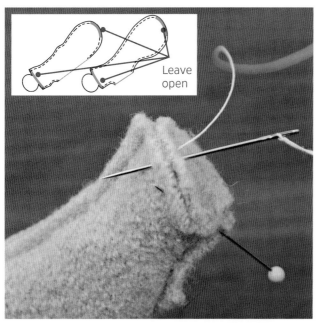

Leave open

10. If desired, strengthen your goat's legs by following the tip on page 78, Strengthen the Legs. The vinyl-coated mesh or interfacing should be 3" (7.6cm) squares for the goat. Leave an opening at the top, as well, if this step is taken (inset). Stuff the leg firmly with your choice of stuffing. Fold the foot flap over and pin it closed. Hand stitch the foot flap.

11. Pin the completed legs in position on the meadow goat's body. Check the position by standing the goat up and adjusting the leg positions as needed. With a button on the outside of the legs, sew through all layers with a doll needle and doubled heavy thread.

PATTERNS

*Copy page at 100%

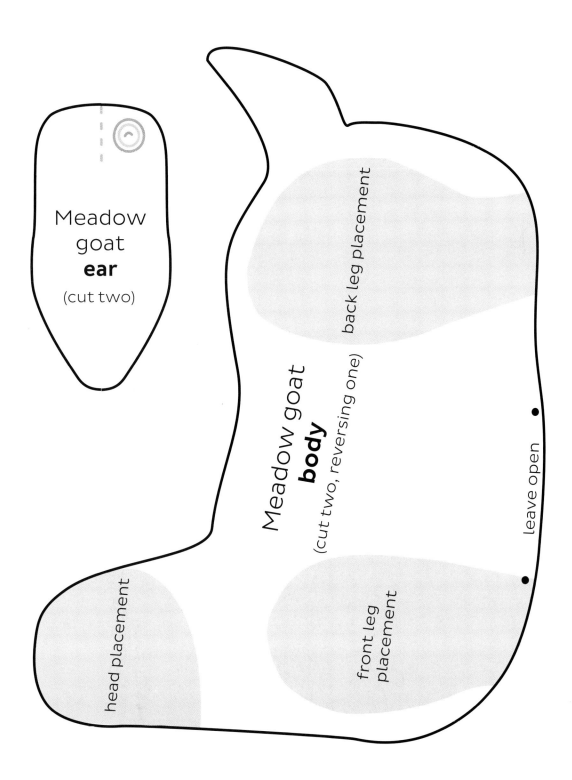

Meadow goat
ear
(cut two)

back leg placement

Meadow goat
body
(cut two, reversing one)

leave open

head placement

front leg
placement

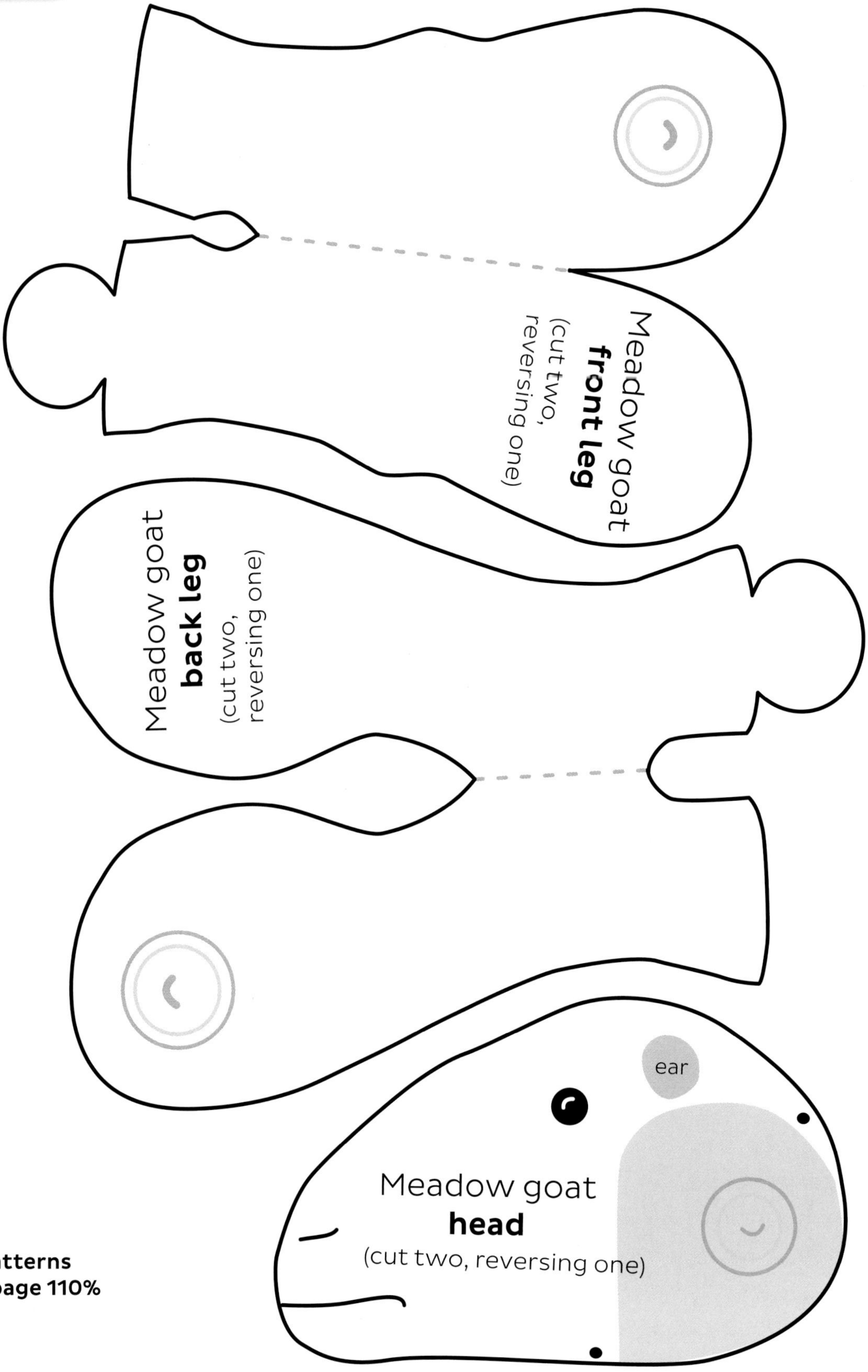

Meadow goat
front leg
(cut two, reversing one)

Meadow goat
back leg
(cut two, reversing one)

ear

Meadow goat
head
(cut two, reversing one)

*Scale patterns
on this page 110%

MOUNTAIN GOAT

The mountain goat is made in much the same manner as the meadow goat, with the exception of the added horns.

SUPPLIES

- ⅓ yd. (30.48cm) or 12" × 24" (30.50 × 61cm) felted wool fabric
- 3" × 3" (7.6 × 7.6cm) felted wool fabric, for horns
- Buttons:
  - Two 1" to 1¼" (25 to 32mm) buttons, for back legs
  - Two ¾" to 1" (19 to 25mm) buttons, for front legs
  - Two ⅝" to ¾" (16 to 19mm) buttons, for head
  - Two ⅜" to ½" (10 to 13mm) buttons, for ears
  - Two ¼" (6mm) buttons, for eyes

- Large straight pins
- Large hand-sewing needle
- 5" (127mm) doll (soft sculpture) needle
- Heavy thread or pearl cotton for hand stitching, or sewing thread for machine stitching
- Pearl cotton or embroidery floss, for embroidering features
- Wool roving, polyester fiberfill, or wool scraps
- Chopstick or stuffing tool
- Freezer paper (optional)

1. Follow steps 1 to 4 from the Meadow Goat project (see pages 94 to 95), then cut out the horns from a slightly darker shade of wool. Fold each horn tip in half toward the center with *wrong* sides facing and stitch. See the stitching map for the horns, above.

2. Pin the horns to the *back of head* piece with the *wrong* side of the horns to the *right* side of the head back. Stitch the edge to secure.

3. Lay the front of head piece over the joined horns/back-of-head piece, overlapping the back piece. Stitch across the horn section. Then pull the sides together and pin, overlapping by ⅜" (10mm), and stitch. See the stitching map for assembling the horned head, right.

4. Fold the head in half with *wrong* sides facing, and pin. Stitch around the nose and the top of the head ⅛" (3.18mm) from the edge. Leave the neck edge open for stuffing. Finish the mountain goat by following steps 5 to 11 on pages 95 to 96.

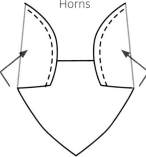

Horns

Fold horn tips toward
the center and stitch

Assembling head

Sew horn overlap area first

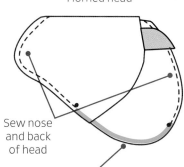

Horned head

Sew nose
and back
of head

Leave open

PATTERNS

*Copy page at 100%

Mountain goat
horns
(cut one)

Mountain goat
back of head
(cut one)

ear

Mountain goat
front of head
(cut one)

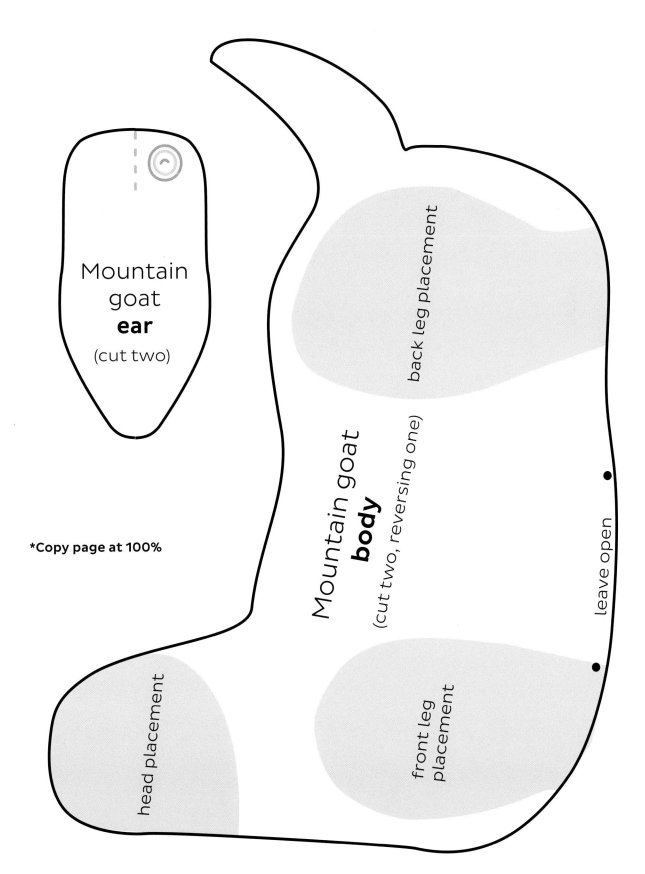

Mountain
goat
ear

(cut two)

*Copy page at 100%

Mountain goat
body

(cut two, reversing one)

back leg placement

leave open

head placement

front leg
placement

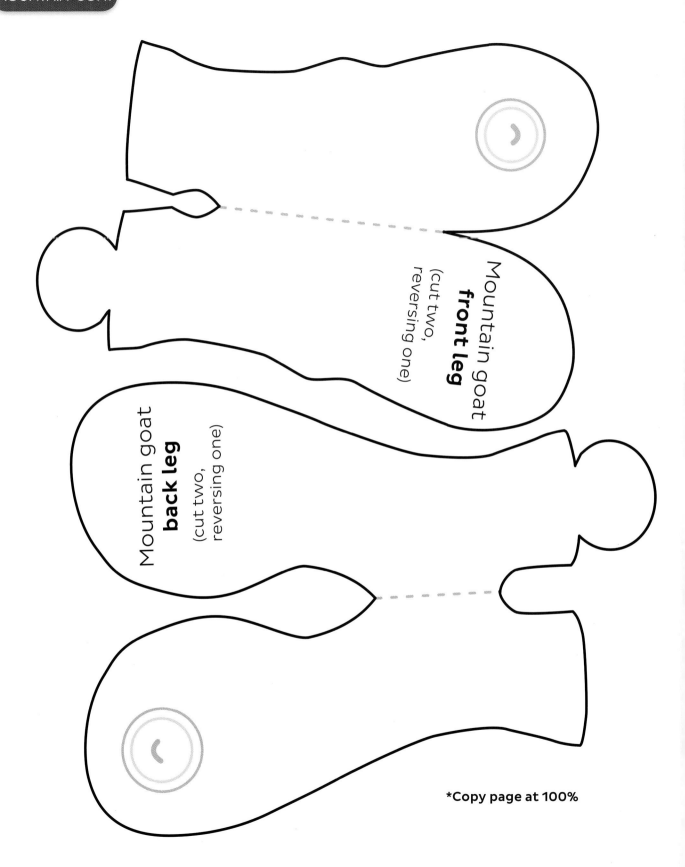

MOUNTAIN GOAT

Mountain goat **front leg**
(cut two, reversing one)

Mountain goat **back leg**
(cut two, reversing one)

*Copy page at 100%

WOOLLY SHEEP

What animal could be more appropriate for a felted wool project than a sheep? As the source of all things woolen, this animal gets an extra shaggy coat made with loops of yarn. Black, brown, tan, and white are natural colors for sheep, but have fun with multicolored spotted or plaid wool as well. Posable ears and legs give this sheep plenty of personality.

SUPPLIES

- ⅓ yd. (30.48cm) or 10" × 24" (25.4 × 61cm) felted wool fabric
- Buttons:
  - Two 1" to 1¼" (25 to 32mm) buttons, for back legs
  - Two ¾" to 1" (19 to 25mm) buttons, for front legs
  - Two ⅜" to ½" (10 to 13mm) buttons, for ears
  - Two ¼" (6mm) buttons, for eyes
- Large straight pins
- Large hand-sewing needle

- 5" (127mm) doll (soft sculpture) needle
- Heavy thread or pearl cotton for hand stitching, or sewing thread for machine stitching
- Pearl cotton or embroidery floss, for embroidering features
- Yarn, for fleece
- Wool roving, polyester fiberfill, or wool scraps
- Chopstick or stuffing tool
- Permanent marker
- Freezer paper (optional)

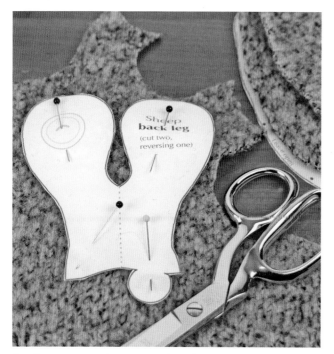

1. Prepare and cut out the sheep pattern pieces. Pin the pattern pieces to a single layer of wool and cut out, reversing the patterns as indicated, or cut around the freezer paper patterns.

2. Pin the body pieces together with *wrong* sides facing. Stitch around the body ⅛" (3.18mm) from the edge; leave an opening for stuffing. See the stitching map for the body, below.

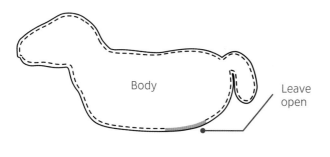

Body

Leave open

3. Firmly fill the body with stuffing. Begin with small pieces in the tail. Use a chopstick to push in the stuffing and to manipulate the shape. When the body is filled firmly, pin and hand stitch the opening closed.

Legs

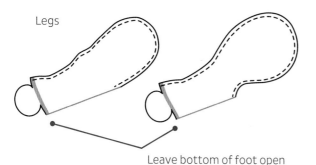

Leave bottom of foot open

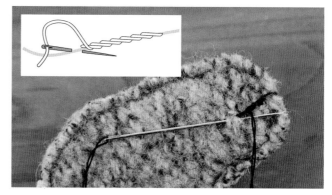

4. Embroider the mouth and nose using black pearl cotton or embroidery floss. Lightly mark the features with a permanent marker. Work a stem stitch as shown in the inset.

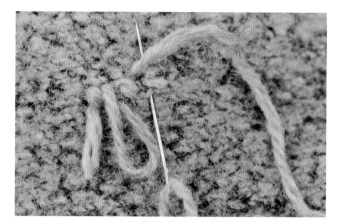

7. Stitch through the fabric and leave the next stitch in a ½" (1.27cm) loop. Pull the following stitch tight to lock the loop. Continue, pulling the yarn tight between each loose stitch.

5. Assemble the legs. Fold each leg in half with *wrong* sides facing and pin. Using a ⅛" (3.18mm) seam allowance, stitch the leg as far as the foot. See the stitching map for the legs, below opposite. For optional leg stiffening, follow the directions on page 78.

8. Leave the head unstitched as well as the areas of the body that will be covered by the legs.

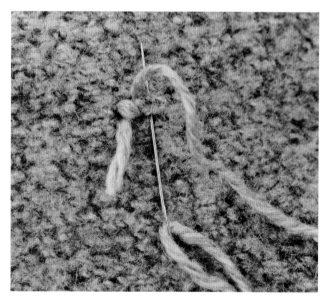

6. To make a woolly sheep, you'll have to hand stitch loops with yarn. Cover the body, neck, and the top of the legs with loops. Leave the areas for the face, leg, and button placement clear. Begin by threading a long piece of yarn on a large eye needle. Stitch through the fabric, pulling the yarn to leave a ½" (1.27cm) loose end. Take a second stitch close to the first and pull the yarn tight.

9. On the legs, stitch yarn loops only on the top section that faces away from the body. Leave the areas that will be covered by the buttons bare.

10. Stuff the legs firmly. Fold the foot flap over and pin it closed. Hand stitch the foot flap closed.

11. Fold each ear with *wrong* sides facing and pin it in place on each side of the head. Place a button on each side, and stitch through the head to secure the ears. Sew ¼" (6mm)–diameter buttons in place for eyes. Stitch through the head, pulling the doubled thread to indent the head slightly.

12. Pin the completed legs in position on the body. Check the position by standing the sheep up. Adjust the leg positions as needed.

13. Place a button on either side of a pair of legs, and sew through all layers with a doll needle and pearl cotton or doubled heavy thread. Pull the legs tight to the body.

PATTERNS

*Copy page at 100%

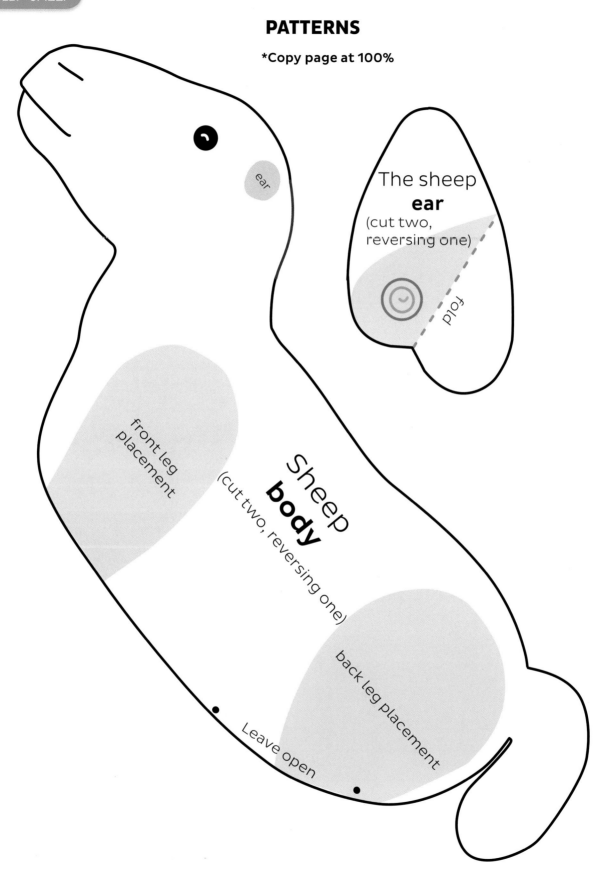

ear

The sheep
ear
(cut two,
reversing one)

fold

**Sheep
body**
(cut two, reversing one)

front leg
placement

back leg placement

Leave open

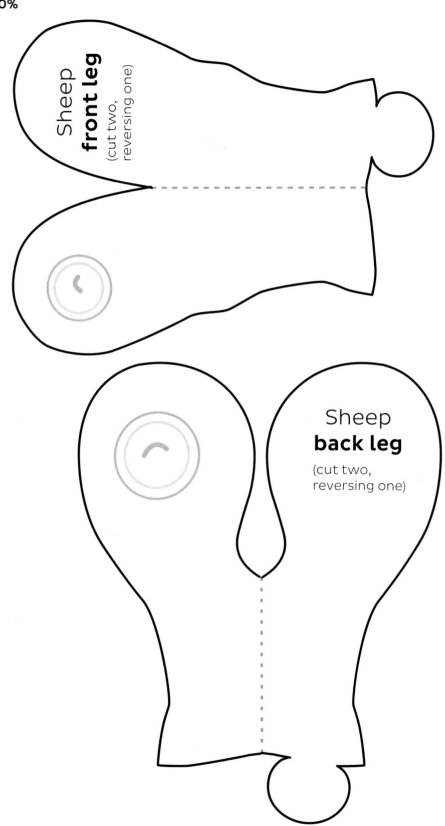

Sheep
front leg

(cut two,
reversing one)

Sheep
back leg

(cut two,
reversing one)

WILD ORCA

As part of the dolphin family, the orca is famously intelligent and playful. This pattern beautifully displays its distinctive markings and its upright dorsal fin. Kids will love this orca, right down to its button-jointed fins.

SUPPLIES

- ¼ yd. (22.86cm) or 9" × 15" (22.8 × 38.1cm) black felted wool
- ¼ yd. (22.86cm) or 5" × 9" (12.7 × 22.8cm) white felted wool
- Buttons:
  - Two ⅜" to ½" (10 to 13mm) buttons, for fins
  - Two ¼" (6mm) buttons or two ¼" or ⅜" (6 or 10mm) beads, for eyes
- Large straight pins
- Large hand-sewing needle
- 5" (127mm) doll (soft sculpture) needle
- Heavy thread or pearl cotton for hand stitching, or sewing thread for machine stitching
- Wool roving, polyester fiberfill, or wool scraps
- Chopstick or stuffing tool
- Freezer paper (optional)

Dorsal fin

Fluke

Pectoral fin

1. Prepare and cut out the orca pattern pieces. Pin the pattern pieces to the wool and cut out, reversing the patterns as indicated, or cut around the freezer paper patterns.

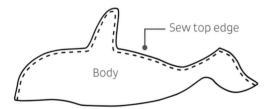

Sew top edge

Body

Sew half of the belly to the body at a time

Belly

Leave open

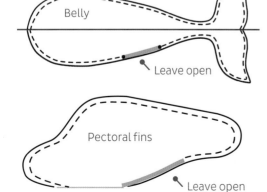

Pectoral fins

Leave open

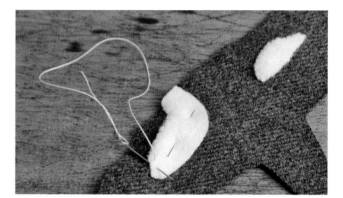

2. Appliqué the spots to both pieces of the orca's body. Use a thread color that matches the spots.

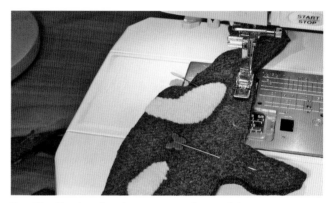

3. Pin the body pieces together with *wrong* sides facing. Stitch across the back ⅛" (3.18mm) from the edge. See the stitching map for the body, left.

4. Open the orca's body and pin one side of it to the belly with *wrong* sides facing. Using matching thread, stitch around the belly ⅛" (3.18mm) from the edge. Sew one side at a time and leave an opening to stuff. See the stitching map for the belly, below left.

5. Very lightly stuff the fluke with small pieces of stuffing. Then firmly fill the rest of the body. Work small pieces into the dorsal fin. Use a chopstick to push them in and manipulate the shape. When firm, hand stitch the opening closed.

6. Fold and pin the pectoral fin pieces together with *wrong* sides facing. Stitch around each fin ⅛" (3.18mm) from the edge. Leave an opening to stuff. See the stitching map for the pectoral fins, left.

7. Very lightly stuff the pectoral fins and sew the openings closed. Pin the fins to the orca's body. With a button on either side, sew through all layers with a doll needle and doubled heavy thread or pearl cotton.

8. Sew beads or buttons in place for eyes. Stitch through the body and pull the doubled thread to indent the body slightly.

PATTERNS

*Copy page at 100%

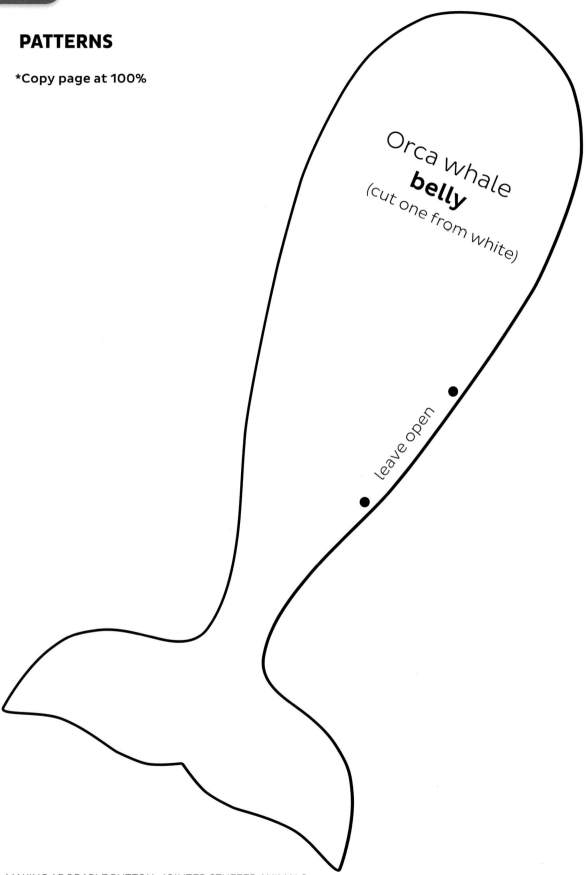

Orca whale
belly
(cut one from white)

leave open

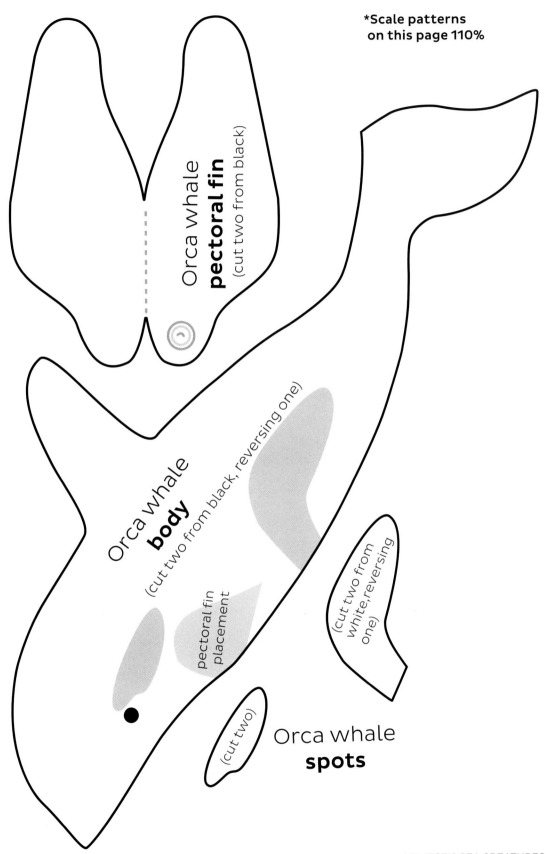

*Scale patterns
on this page 110%

Orca whale
pectoral fin
(cut two from black)

Orca whale
body
(cut two from black, reversing one)

(cut two from
white, reversing
one)

pectoral fin
placement

(cut two)

Orca whale
spots

SPERM WHALE

This figure not only captures the classic whale look, it is one of the simplest patterns in this book to make. These steps include embroidering the eyes or using circles of wool instead of buttons to make a toy suitable for a very young child.

SUPPLIES

- ⅓ yd. (30.48cm) or 12" × 25" (30.5 × 63.5cm) felted wool fabric
- Buttons:
  - Two ⅜" to ½" (10 to 13mm) buttons, for fins
  - Two ¼" (6mm) buttons or two ¼" or ⅜" (6 or 10mm) beads, for eyes
- Large straight pins
- Large hand-sewing needle

- 5" (127mm) doll (soft sculpture) needle
- Heavy thread or pearl cotton for hand stitching, or sewing thread for machine stitching
- Wool roving, polyester fiberfill, or wool scraps
- Chopstick or stuffing tool
- Freezer paper (optional)

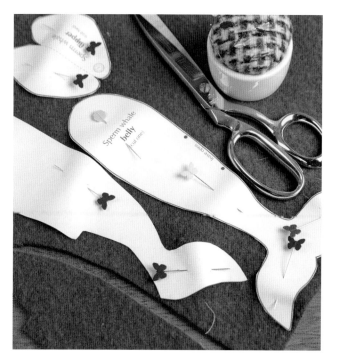

1. Prepare and cut out the sperm whale pattern pieces. Pin the pattern pieces to the wool and cut out, reversing the patterns as indicated, or cut around the freezer paper patterns.

2. Pin the body pieces together with *wrong* sides facing. Stitch across the back ⅛" (3.18mm) from the edge. See the stitching map for the body, below.

3. Open the whale's body and pin it with *wrong* sides facing the belly. Pin and sew one side at a time. Stitch around the belly ⅛" (3.18mm) from the edge. Leave an opening to stuff. See the stitching map for the belly, left.

Sew top edge

Body

Sew half of the belly to the body at a time

Belly

Leave open

Pectoral fins

Leave open

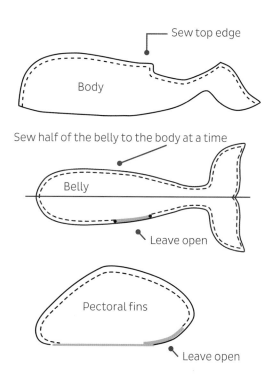

4. Mark the stitching lines across the fluke with pins and stitch along them. Begin stuffing the sperm whale with small pieces pushed into the pectoral fin and the center section of the fluke.

5. Firmly fill the body with stuffing. Use a chopstick to push pieces in and to manipulate the shape. When firm, hand stitch the opening closed.

6. Fold and pin the pectoral fin pieces together with *wrong* sides facing. Stitch around each fin ⅛" (3.18mm) from the edge. Leave an opening to stuff. See the stitching map for the pectoral fins, below left.

7. Very lightly stuff the pectoral fins and sew the openings closed. Pin a pectoral fin to either side of the whale's body. With a button on either side, sew through all layers with a doll needle and doubled heavy thread or pearl cotton.

8. If your whale is for a young child, embroider the eyes using a doubled strand of pearl cotton, or sew beads or buttons in place for eyes. In either case, stitch through the body, pulling the thread to indent the body slightly.

PATTERNS

*Copy page at 100%

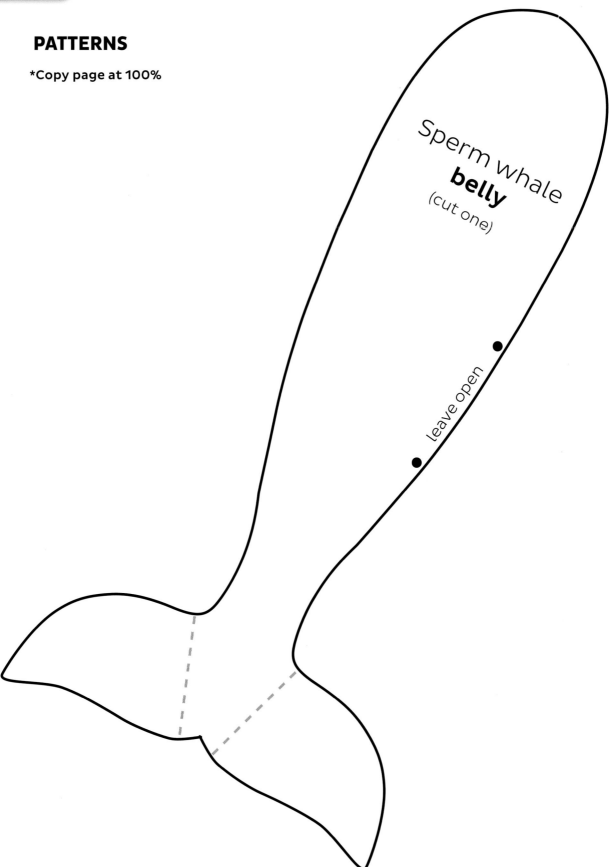

Sperm whale **belly** (cut one)

leave open

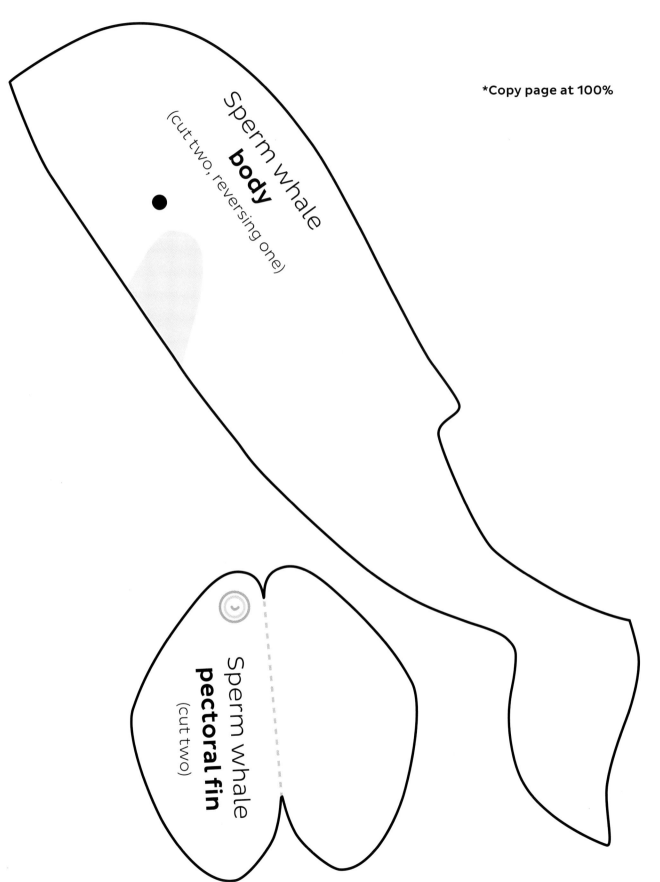

*Copy page at 100%

Sperm whale
body
(cut two, reversing one)

Sperm whale
pectoral fin
(cut two)

SEA TURTLE

With a button-jointed head and flippers, this sea turtle is ready to explore the open sea. In the wild, sea turtles are green or black with yellow bellies, but reds, blues, and purples look great, too. Consider using patterned felted wool to capture the mottled colors of the shell and flippers. Use a heavyweight felted fabric for the shell.

SUPPLIES

- Felted wool
  - ¼ yd. (22.86cm) or 7" × 8" (17.8 × 20.32cm), for top shell
  - ¼ yd. (22.86cm) or 6" × 7" (15.24 × 17.8cm), for bottom shell
  - ¼ yd. (22.86cm) or 9" × 20" (22.86 × 50.8cm), for body and head
- Buttons:
  - Six ½" (13mm) buttons, for head and front flippers
  - Two ¼" or ⅜" (6 or 10mm) buttons, for eyes

- Large straight pins
- Large hand-sewing needle
- Heavy thread or pearl cotton for hand stitching, or sewing thread for machine stitching
- Pearl cotton or embroidery floss, for shell embroidery and mouth
- Wool roving, polyester fiberfill, or wool scraps
- Chopstick or stuffing tool
- Permanent marker
- Freezer paper (optional)

Body

Head

Flippers

Leave open

Leave open

Leave open

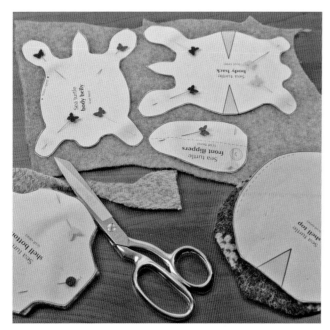

1. Prepare and cut out the sea turtle pattern pieces. Pin the pattern pieces to the wool and cut out, reversing the patterns as indicated, or cut around the freezer paper patterns.

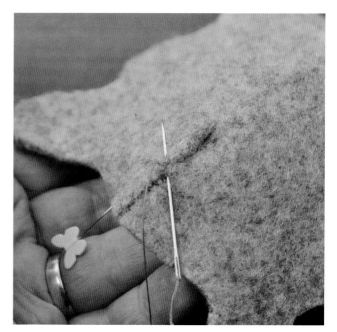

2. Clip along one side of each dart triangle of the *body back* piece. Overlap the shaded area and pin. Stitch the dart closed with matching thread.

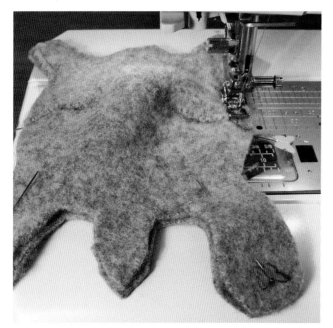

3. Pin the body pieces together with *wrong* sides facing. Stitch around the body ⅛" (3.18mm) from the edge; leave an opening for stuffing.

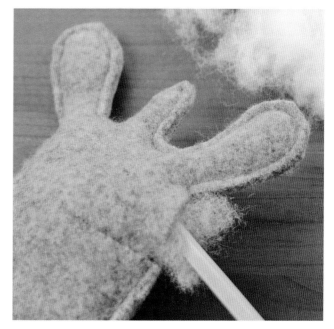

4. Firmly fill the body with stuffing. Begin by putting small pieces in the tail. Use a chopstick to push them in and manipulate the shape. Lightly fill the back fins but don't put stuffing in the front fin.

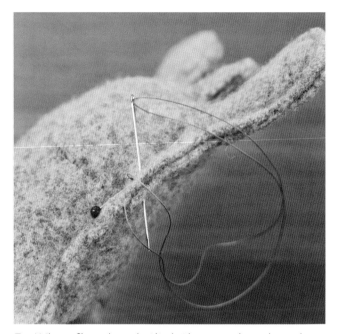

5. When firm, hand stitch the opening closed.

6. Pin the head piece together with *wrong* sides facing. Stitch around the head ⅛" (3.18mm) from the edge; leave the end opening for stuffing. See the stitching map for the body on page 125.

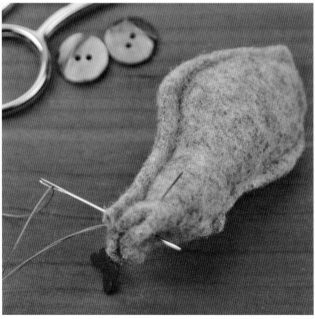

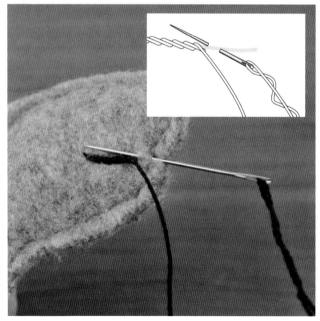

7. Stuff the head firmly. Leave the last ½" (13mm) of the neck unstuffed. Pin the neck closed with the seam in the center of the top edge. Stitch the opening closed.

8. Embroider the mouth, using black pearl cotton or embroidery floss. Lightly mark the features with a permanent marker. Work a stem stitch (inset).

9. Sew ¼" or ⅜" (6 or 10mm) buttons in place for eyes. Stitch through the head, pulling the doubled thread to indent the head slightly.

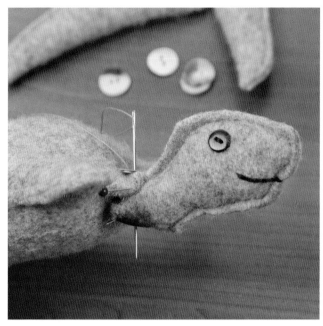

10. Pin the head under the body neck bump. Placing a button on the top of the neck and the bottom of the head, sew through all layers with doubled heavy thread or pearl cotton.

11. Pin the flipper pieces in half with *wrong* sides facing. Stitch around the edge ⅛" (3.18mm) from the edge. Leave the large area open to stuff. See the stitching map for the flippers, page 125.

12. Very lightly stuff the flippers and sew the opening closed. Pin the flippers to the body, overlapping the forearms. With a button on the top and bottom, sew through all layers with doubled heavy thread or pearl cotton.

13. Clip along one side of each dart triangle of the *shell top* piece. Overlap the shaded area and pin. Stitch the dart closed with matching thread.

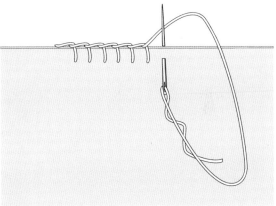

14. Embroider the outer edge of the shell top, using pearl cotton or embroidery floss. Work a blanket stitch (above).

15. Pin the shell top to the shell bottom along the sides. Overlap the top slightly. Stitch them together. Loosely tack the two at the neckline and at the tail area.

PATTERNS

***Scale patterns
on this page 110%**

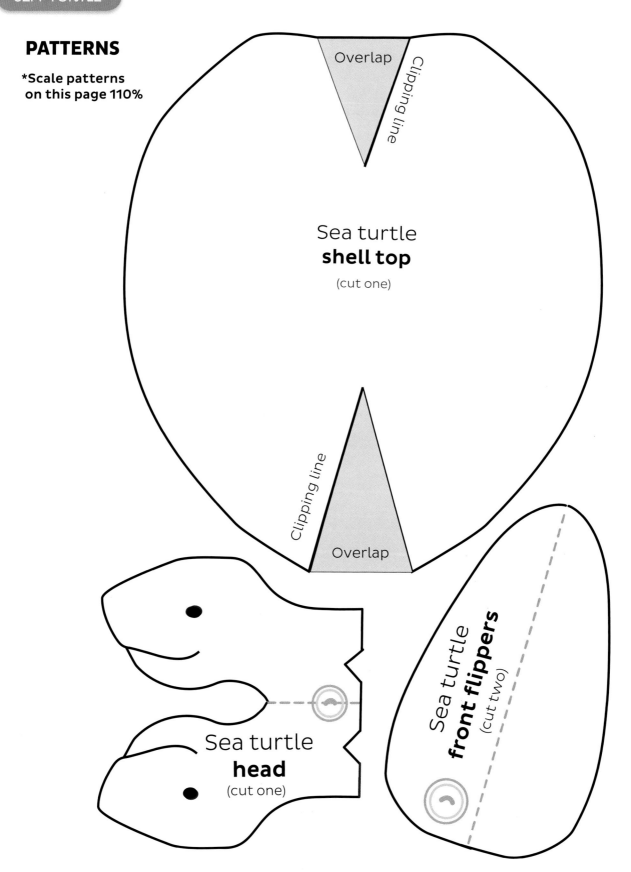

Overlap

Clipping line

Sea turtle
shell top
(cut one)

Clipping line

Overlap

Sea turtle
head
(cut one)

Sea turtle
front flippers
(cut two)

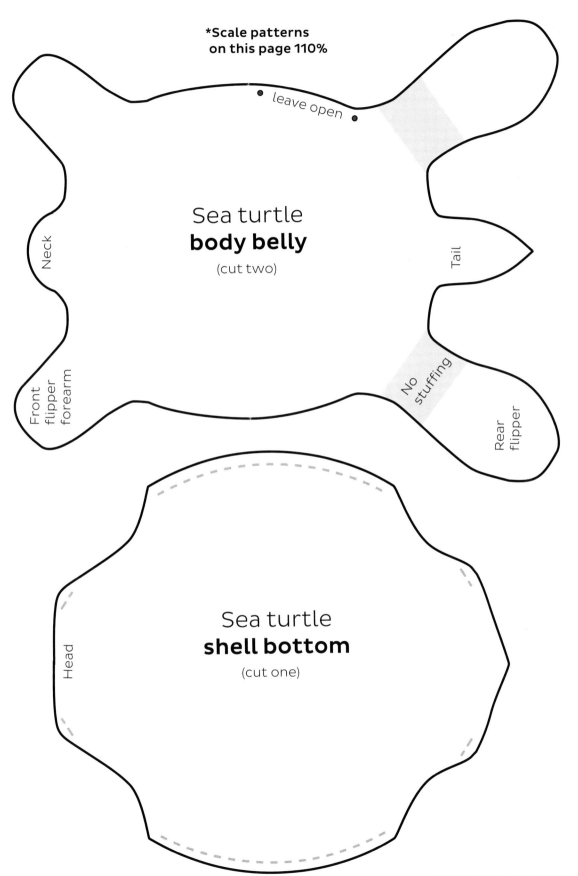

*Scale patterns
on this page 110%

leave open

Sea turtle
body belly
(cut two)

Neck

Tail

Front flipper forearm

No stuffing

Rear flipper

Sea turtle
shell bottom
(cut one)

Head

*Copy page at 100%

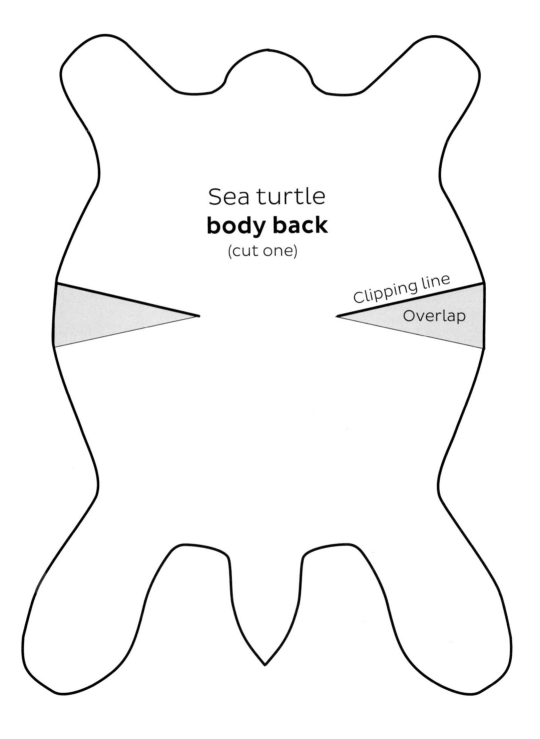

Sea turtle
body back
(cut one)

Clipping line

Overlap

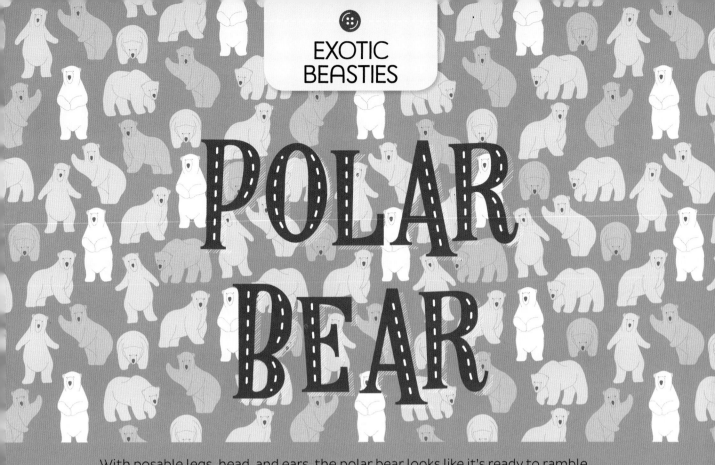

EXOTIC BEASTIES

POLAR BEAR

With posable legs, head, and ears, the polar bear looks like it's ready to ramble across the Arctic. Feel free to get adventurous with the color on this one—though essentially white, polar bears tend to take on a yellow, orange, or even pink color depending on the time of day. Although this button-jointed animal has multiple parts, each is simple to make and the whole thing goes together easily.

SUPPLIES

- ⅓ yd. (30.48cm) or 12" × 30" (30.5 × 76.2cm) felted wool fabric
- Buttons:
  - Four ¾" to 1¼" (19 to 32mm) buttons, for legs
  - Two ⅝" to ¾" (16 to 19mm) buttons, for head
  - Two ⅜" to ½" (10 to 13mm) buttons, for ears
  - Two ¼" (6mm) buttons, for eyes
- Large straight pins
- Large hand-sewing needle
- 5" to 6" (127 to 152mm) doll (soft sculpture) needle
- Heavy thread or pearl cotton for hand stitching, or sewing thread for machine stitching
- Wool roving, polyester fiberfill, or wool scraps
- Chopstick or stuffing tool
- Freezer paper (optional)

1. Prepare and cut out the pattern pieces. Pin the pattern pieces to the wool and cut out, reversing the patterns as indicated, or cut around the freezer paper patterns.

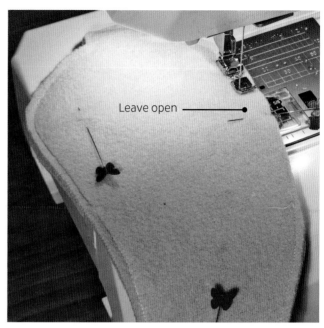

2. Pin the body pieces together with *wrong* sides facing. Stitch around the body ⅛" (3.18mm) from the edge; leave an opening for stuffing.

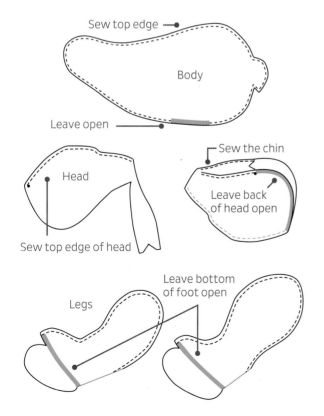

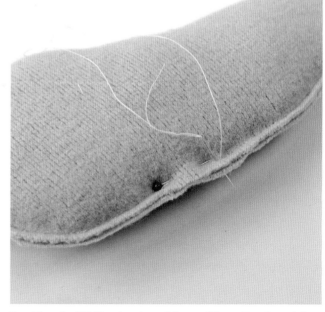

3. Firmly fill the body with stuffing. Begin with small pieces in the tail. Use a chopstick to push in the stuffing and manipulate the shape. When the body is filled firmly, pin and hand stitch the opening closed.

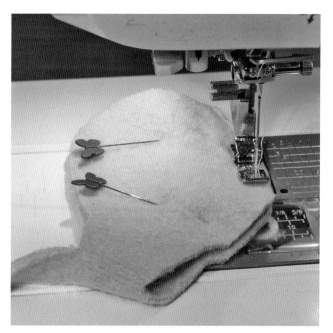

4. Fold the head at the nose with *wrong* sides facing; stitch the top of the head from the dot to the nose. Leave the neck area open between the dots. See the stitching map for the head, page 134.

5. Fold the chin piece under, pinning it to one side of the lower head; stitch from the dot to the nose. Then repeat to sew the other side. Set the head aside.

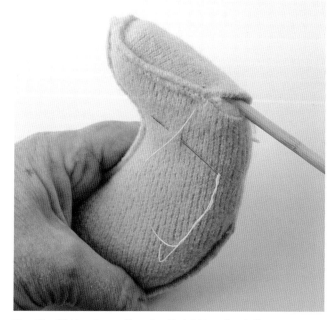

6. Assemble the legs. Fold each leg in half with *wrong* sides facing and pin. Stitch the edges of the leg as far as the foot. See the stitching map for the legs, page 134.

7. Stuff the legs firmly. Fold the foot flap over and pin it closed. Hand stitch the toe and side of the foot flap. Leave the heel open. Add stuffing to shape the foot nicely, then stitch the rest of the flap closed.

8. Fill the front two-thirds of the head with your choice of stuffing.

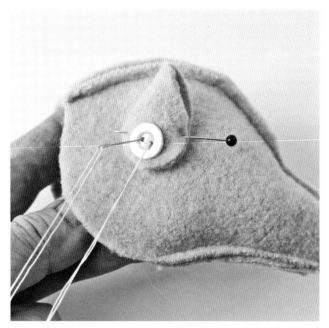

9. Fold an ear in half and, referring to the placement markings, pin one to each side of the head. Stitch each ear to the head with a button. Do not stitch through the head. Place the head in position on the body; pin. Add stuffing as needed to give the head a pleasing shape.

10. Pin the completed legs in position on the body. Stand the polar bear on all four legs. Adjust the legs so it stands evenly. Hold a button on either side of a pair of legs. Sew through the body and buttons with a doll needle and pearl cotton or doubled heavy thread. In the same manner, sew the head to the body.

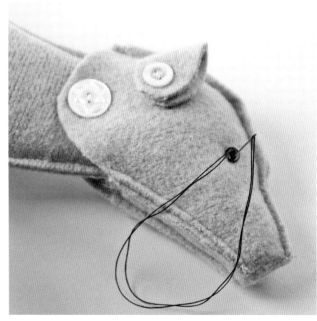

11. Sew ¼" (6mm) buttons in place for eyes. Stitch through the head with doubled thread, pulling to indent the head slightly.

POLAR BEAR

PATTERNS

*Copy page at 100%

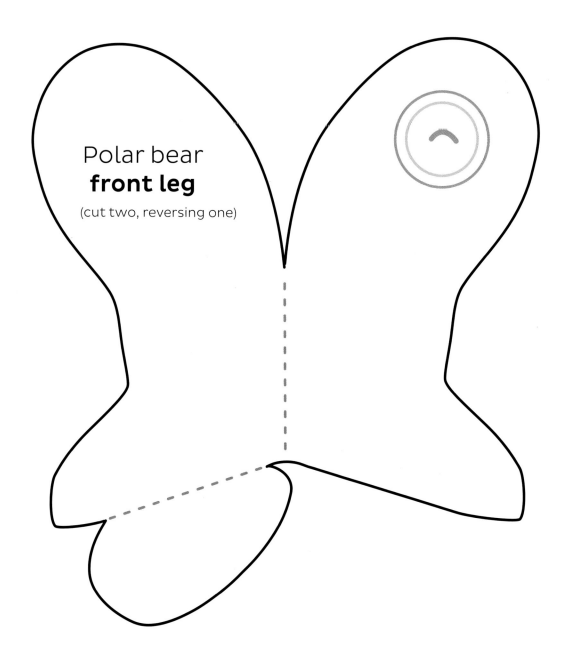

Polar bear
front leg

(cut two, reversing one)

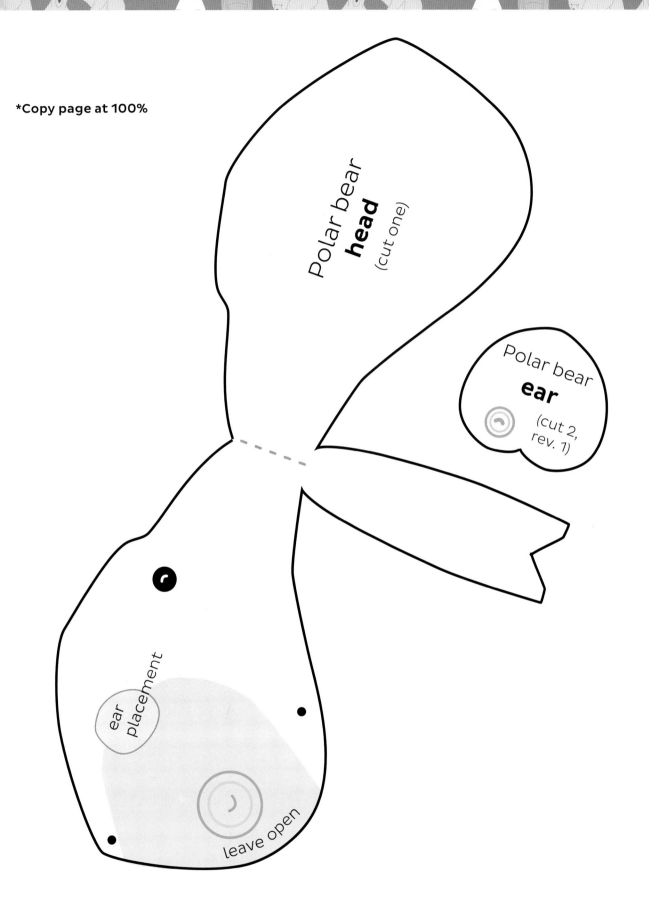

*Copy page at 100%

Polar bear **head** (cut one)

Polar bear **ear** (cut 2, rev. 1)

ear placement

leave open

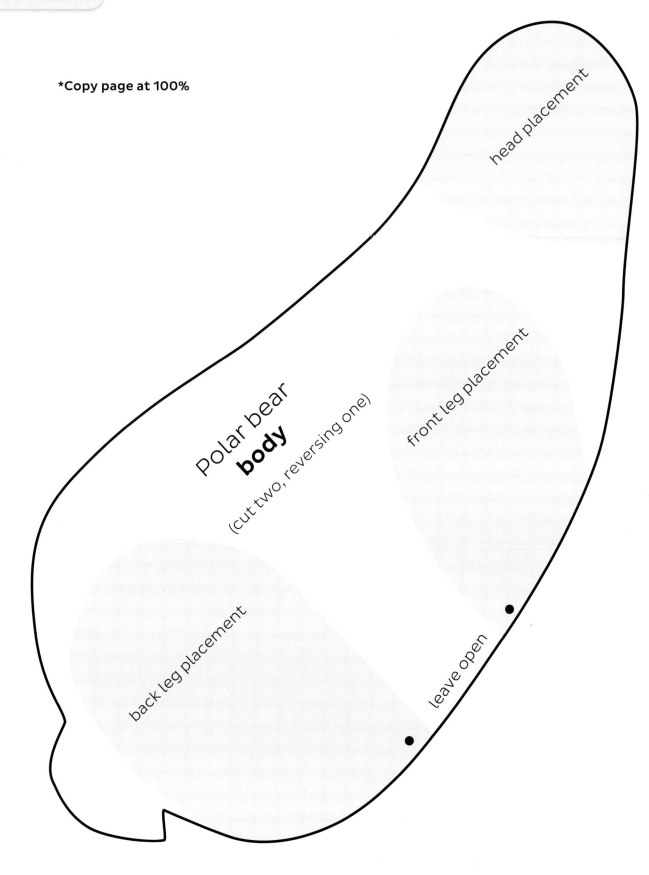

*Copy page at 100%

head placement

Polar bear
body
(cut two, reversing one)

front leg placement

back leg placement

leave open

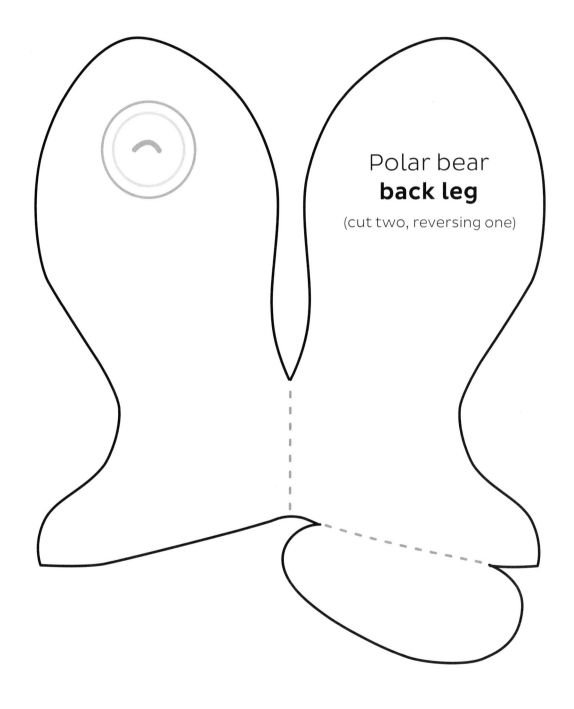

Polar bear
back leg

(cut two, reversing one)

DUSTY CAMEL

This dromedary is standing tall and ready to trek over desert dunes. Felted-wool wonderfully mimics a camel's coat, and though this lanky guy has long legs, medium-weight wool is adequate to hold him up when the legs are stuffed firmly. With an embroidered nose and mouth and a tail made with the ribbed sleeve portion of a felted sweater, this camel offers plenty of personality.

SUPPLIES

- ⅓ yd. (30.48cm) or 12" × 40" (30.5 × 101.6cm) felted wool fabric
- Buttons:
  - Four 1" to 1¼" (25 to 32mm) buttons, for legs
  - Two ⅝" to ¾" (16 to 19mm) buttons, for head
  - Two ⅜" to ½" (10 to 13mm) buttons, for ears
  - Two ¼" (6mm) buttons, for eyes
- Large straight pins
- Large hand-sewing needle

- 5" to 6" (127 to 152mm) doll (soft sculpture) needle
- Heavy thread or pearl cotton for hand stitching, or sewing thread for machine stitching
- Black pearl cotton or embroidery floss, for features
- Wool roving, polyester fiberfill, or wool scraps
- Chopstick or stuffing tool
- Permanent marker
- Freezer paper (optional)

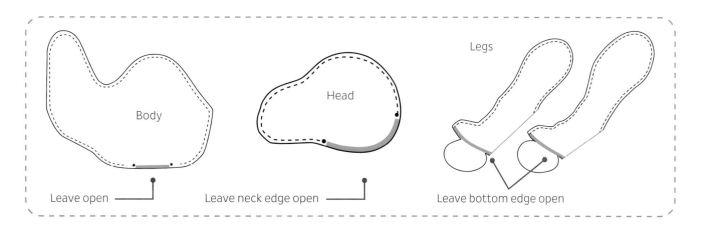

Legs

Body

Head

Leave open

Leave neck edge open

Leave bottom edge open

1. Copy and cut out the camel pattern pieces. Pin the patterns to a single layer of wool and cut out carefully, or cut around the freezer paper patterns. If possible, pin the tail pattern along the ribbed section of the felted sweater and cut out as shown.

2. Fold the tail in half lengthwise with *wrong* sides facing and stitch to the ribbing lines ⅛" (3.18mm) from the edge. Clip between the ridges of the ribbing.

3. Pin the body pieces together with *wrong* sides facing, with the tail in place at the mark. Stitch around the body ⅛" (3.18mm) from the edge; leave an opening for stuffing.

4. Firmly fill the body with stuffing. Use a chopstick to push it in and manipulate the shape. When firm, stitch the opening closed.

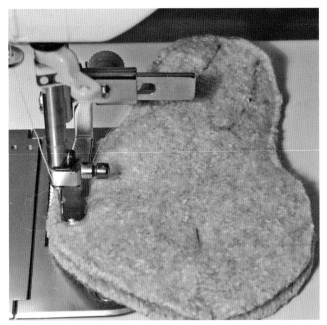

5. Pin the head pieces together with *wrong* sides facing and stitch around the head ⅛" (3.18mm) from the edge. Leave the neck area open between the dots. See the stitching map for the head, page 143.

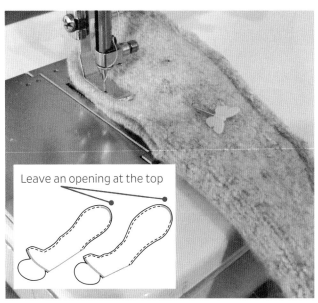

Leave an opening at the top

6. Fold a leg in half with *wrong* sides facing and pin. If you would like your camel to have stiffer legs, follow the tip on page 78. Use 4½" (11.43cm)–square pieces of vinyl-coated mesh or interfacing. Leave an opening at the top of the leg if this step is taken (inset). Stitch around the leg, leaving the foot open. See the stitching map for the leg, page 143. Stuff the legs firmly.

7. Fold the foot flap over and pin it closed. Hand stitch the toe and side. Leave the heel open. Add stuffing to shape the foot nicely, then stitch the rest of the flap closed. Repeat to make the other foot.

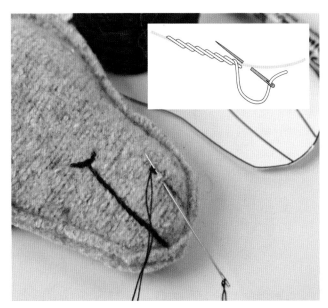

8. Embroider the nose and mouth, using black pearl cotton or embroidery floss. Lightly mark the features with an ultrafine permanent marker. Work a stem stitch as shown.

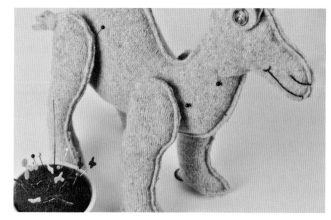

11. Pin the completed legs in position on the body. Stand the camel on all four legs. Adjust the leg positions as needed.

9. Fill the nose and the top half of the head with stuffing. Place the head in position on the body; pin. Add stuffing as needed to give the head a pleasing shape.

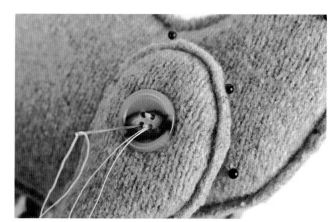

12. With a button on either side of a pair of legs, sew through all layers with a doll needle and pearl cotton or doubled heavy thread. In the same manner, sew the head to the body.

10. Fold each ear with *wrong* sides facing and pin it in place on each side of the head. With a button on each side, stitch through the head to secure the ears. Be careful not to catch the neck in the stitching.

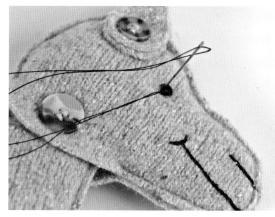

13. Sew ¼" (6mm)–diameter buttons in place for eyes. Stitch through the head, pulling the doubled thread to indent the head slightly.

PATTERNS

*Scale patterns on this page 110%

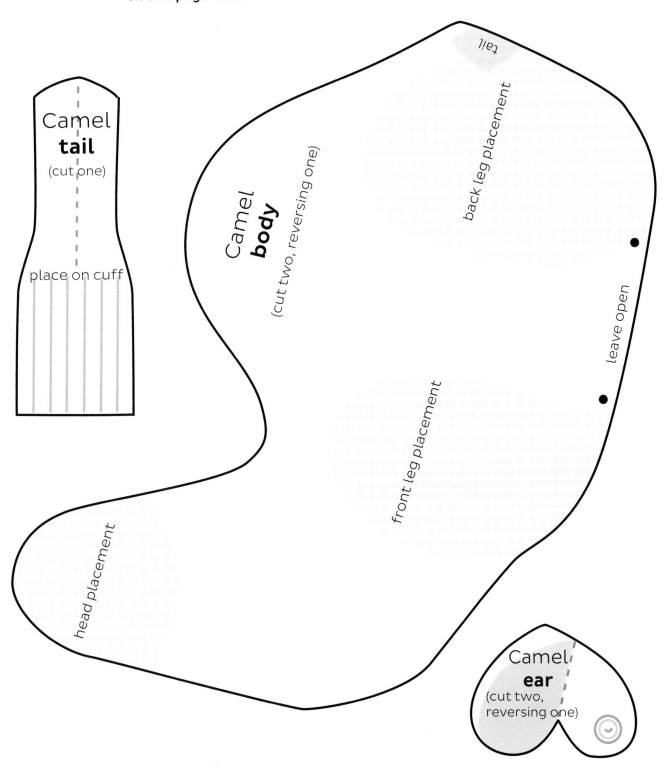

Camel
tail
(cut one)

place on cuff

Camel
body
(cut two, reversing one)

tail

back leg placement

leave open

front leg placement

head placement

Camel
ear
(cut two,
reversing one)

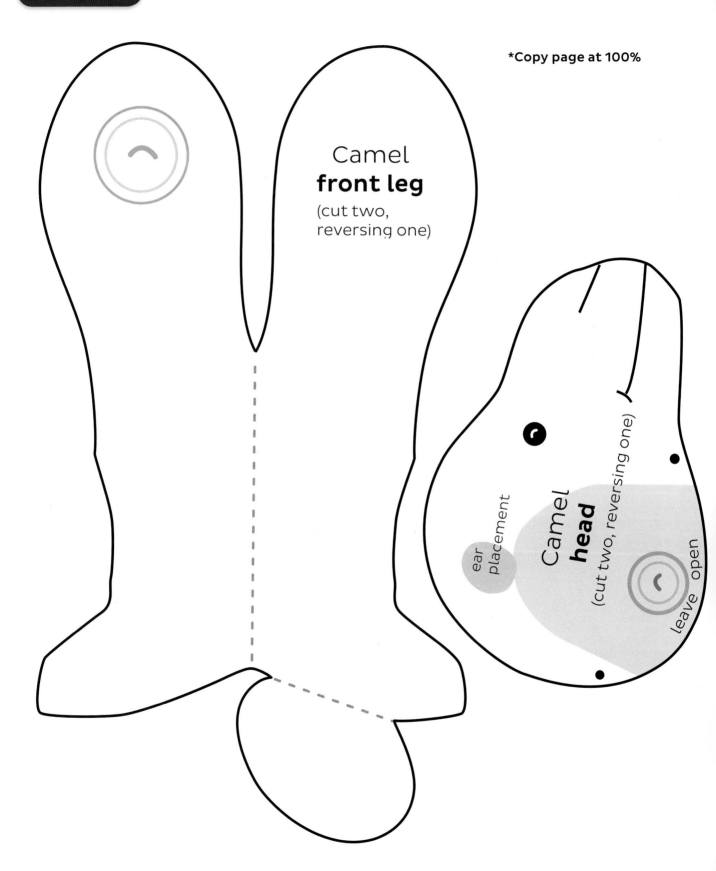

*Copy page at 100%

Camel
front leg
(cut two,
reversing one)

Camel
head
(cut two, reversing one)

ear
placement

leave open

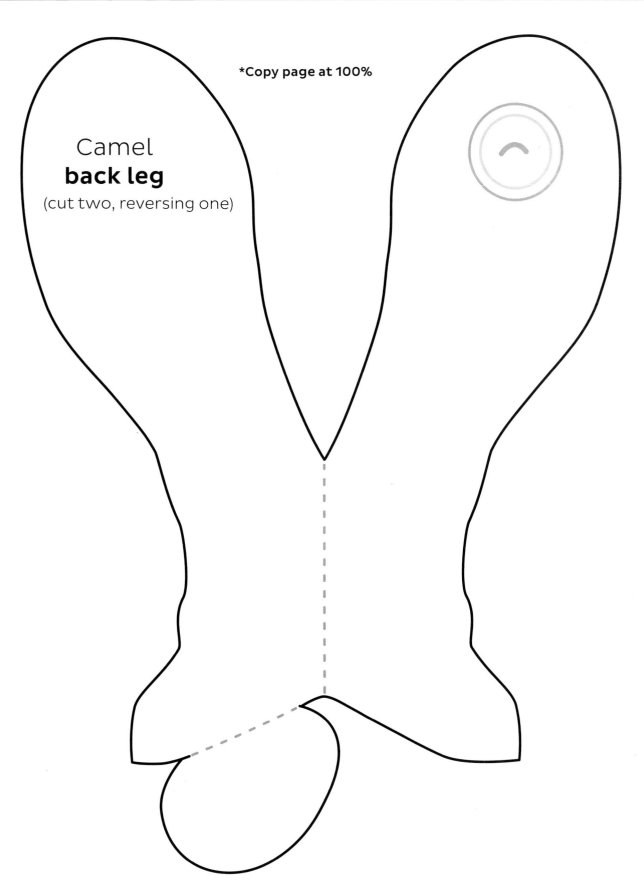

Camel
back leg
(cut two, reversing one)

*Copy page at 100%

FOREST ELF

You have to love this perky scamp! With all the woodland animals in this book, there has to be a woodland elf as well. Here's a great opportunity to gather felted wool pieces of similar hues of green. Pick out a piece of heavyweight wool for his hat. I used the brightest shade for his lively feet.

SUPPLIES

- Felted wool fabric:
  - ¼ yd. (22.86cm) or 9" × 12" (22.8 × 30.5cm), for face and hands
  - ¼ yd. (22.86cm) or 5" × 8" (12.7 × 20.32cm), for hair and cap
  - ¼ yd. (22.86cm) or 9" × 20" (22.8 × 50.8cm), for body, upper limbs, and scarf
  - ¼ yd. (22.86cm) or 7" × 15" (17.78 × 38cm), for feet
- Buttons:
  - Two 1" to 1¼" (25 to 32mm) buttons, for hip joint
  - Four ½" to ¾" (13 to 19mm) buttons, for knee joints
  - Two ⅝" (16mm) buttons, for shoulder joints
  - Four ½" (13mm) buttons, for elbow joints

- Two ¼" (6mm) buttons, for eyes
- Three ¼" to ½" (6 to 13mm) buttons, for cap
- Large straight pins
- Large hand-sewing needle
- 5" (127mm) doll (soft sculpture) needle
- Buttonhole thread or pearl cotton for hand stitching, or sewing thread for machine stitching
- Pearl cotton or embroidery floss to embroider the mouth
- Wool roving, polyester fiberfill, or wool scraps
- Chopstick or stuffing tool
- Freezer paper (optional)

2. Pin the pattern pieces to the wool and cut out, reversing the patterns as indicated, or cut around the freezer paper patterns.

1. Prepare and cut out the elf pattern pieces. I used a variety of colors of felted wool for my elf. Each side of the body is cut from a different (but similar value) of blue green. The head and hands are from the same color of wool.

3. Pin the body pieces together with *wrong* sides facing. Stitch around the body ⅛" (3.18mm) from the edge; leave an opening for stuffing. See the stitching map for the body, opposite.

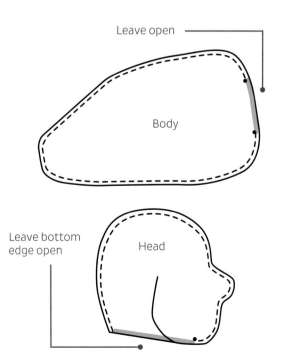

Leave open

Body

Leave bottom edge open

Head

4. Firmly fill the body with stuffing through the bottom opening. Use a chopstick to push the stuffing in and to manipulate the shape. When it is filled firmly, pin and hand stitch the opening closed.

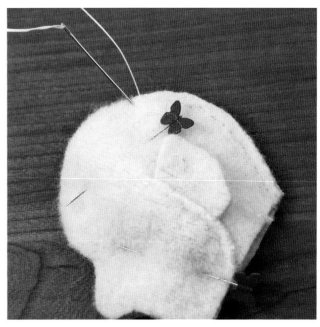

5. Pin the ear in place on the head with the *wrong* side facing the right side of the head. Overlap the cheek on the marking. Stitch along the edge of the slit from the neck edge to the top of the overlap, catching the ear in the seam.

6. After stitching both cheeks, pin the head pieces together with *wrong* sides facing. Stitch around the head ⅛" (3.18mm) from the edge. Leave the neck area open. See the stitching map for the head, opposite.

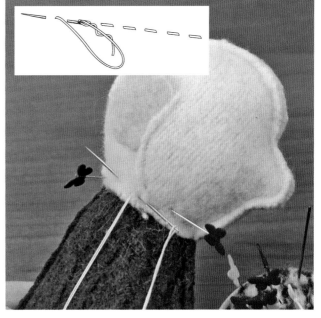

7. Fill the head half full with stuffing and place over the body as marked on the body pattern. Pin the back part of the neck edge to the body. Add stuffing to shape the cheeks and chin; then pin the rest of the neck to the body.

8. Hand stitch the head to the body using a backstitch (inset) with a long needle and doubled heavy thread or pearl cotton. It is not easy to make the stitches close together because of the thickness of the wool, so go around the neck two times, filling in between previous stitches to make a secure seam.

9. Fold the hair around the head and pin it in place. Stitch the hair to the head with matching thread.

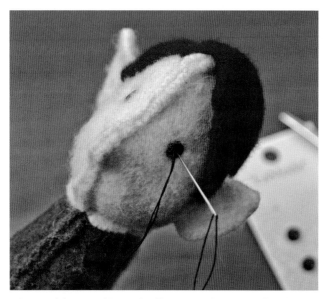

10. Position ¼" (6mm)–diameter buttons in place for the eyes. Stitch through the head, pulling the thread to indent the head slightly, to secure the eyes in place.

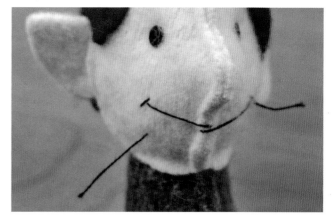

11. As a guide for stitching, use a piece of thread to baste a smile on the elf's face.

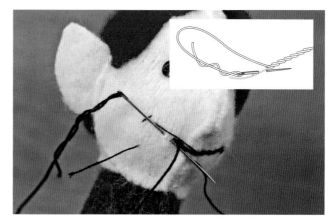

12. Work a stem stitch (inset) to stitch the smile with pearl cotton or floss. Remove the basting thread.

13. Fold each thigh piece in half with *wrong* sides facing and pin. Stitch to the dot, leaving the end open to insert the lower leg. See the stitching map for the upper arm and thigh, opposite.

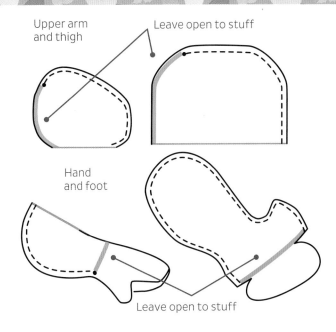

Upper arm and thigh

Leave open to stuff

Hand and foot

Leave open to stuff

14. Firmly fill the thigh pieces three-quarters full with stuffing. Black fiberfill is available and may be a good choice to be less visible at the open end.

15. Pin an inner foot to an outer foot with *wrong* sides facing. Stitch around the foot ⅛" (3.18mm) from the edge, leaving the bottom of the foot open. See the stitching map for hand and foot above right. Fill the leg with stuffing, then fold over the foot flap and pin.

16. Add stuffing to shape the foot, if needed. Hand stitch the foot flap in place. Repeat for the other leg.

17. Insert a foot into each thigh, in a bent knee position. With a button on either side of the knee, sew through all layers with a long needle and doubled heavy thread or pearl cotton.

18. Pin the completed legs in position on the body, lining up the bottom edges of the thighs and the body to allow the elf to sit. With a button on either side, sew through all layers with a doll needle and doubled heavy thread.

19. Assemble the upper arms in the same manner as the thighs. Fold each in half with *wrong* sides facing. Stitch ⅛" (3.18mm) from the edge to the dot. See the stitching map for the upper arm and thigh on page 155. Firmly fill the upper arm pieces three-quarters full with stuffing.

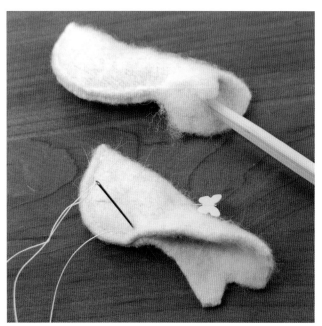

20. Assemble the hand pieces. Fold each in half with *wrong* sides facing. Stitch ⅛" (3.18mm) from the edge to the dot. See the stitching map for the hand and foot on page 155. Firmly fill the forearm with stuffing.

21. After each forearm is stuffed, pin the palms in place. Hand stitch around each one ⅛" (3.18mm) from the edge, leaving an opening to stuff. Very lightly fill the palm and then stitch it closed.

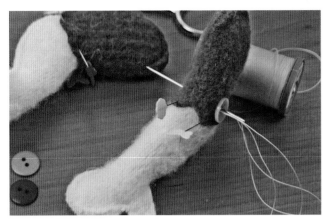

22. Insert the hands into the upper arm pieces, bending the arm at the elbow. Pin in place and stitch each hand to an upper arm with a button on either side.

25. Tack the cap buttons in place with single stitches. Overlap the cap as shown in the pattern markings and put it on the elf to check the size. Adjust as necessary and pin. Then sew the buttons through both layers to secure the shape.

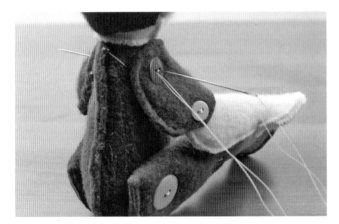

23. Stitch the completed arms to the body with buttons.

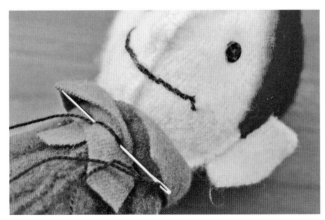

24. Fold the collar along the broken line and wrap it around the elf's neck. Overlap the ends and use pearl cotton or heavy thread to stitch the collar in place.

26. Put the cap on the elf and stitch it to his head at the center back and behind each ear, if desired.

PATTERNS

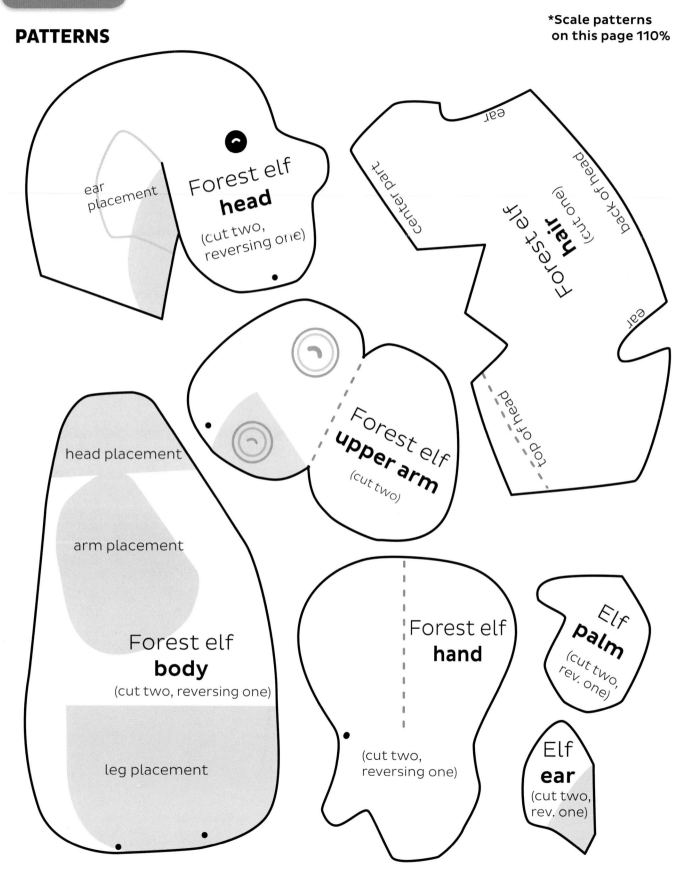

**Forest elf
head**
(cut two,
reversing one)

ear
placement

Forest elf
hair
(cut one)
back of head
ear
ear
center part
top of head

Forest elf
upper arm
(cut two)

head placement

arm placement

**Forest elf
body**
(cut two, reversing one)

leg placement

Forest elf
hand

(cut two,
reversing one)

Elf
palm
(cut two,
rev. one)

Elf
ear
(cut two,
rev. one)

*Scale patterns on this page 110%

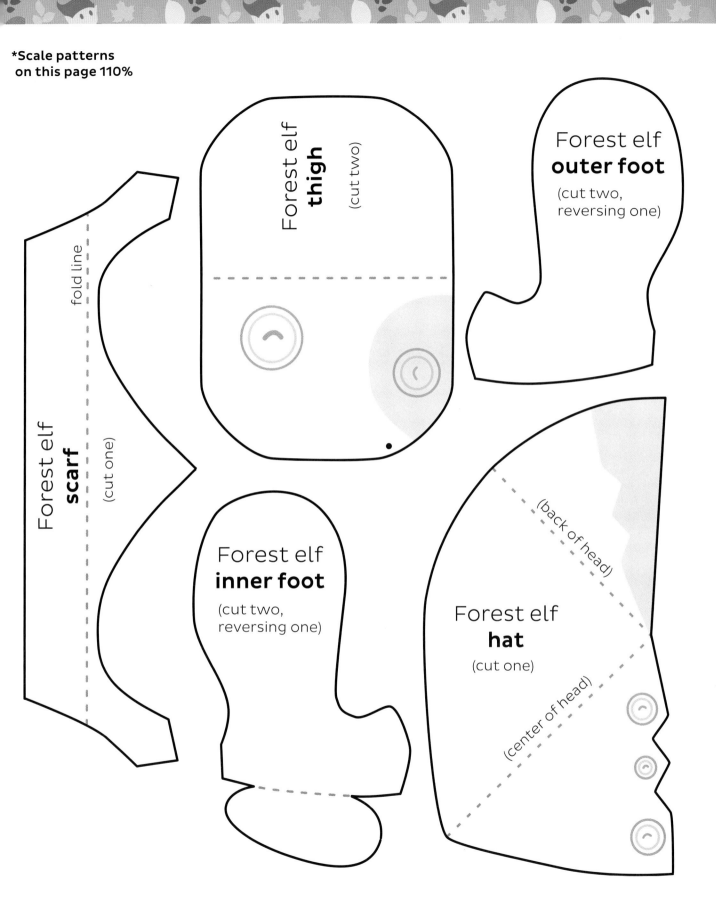

Forest elf **scarf**

(cut one)

fold line

Forest elf **thigh**

(cut two)

Forest elf **outer foot**

(cut two, reversing one)

Forest elf **inner foot**

(cut two, reversing one)

Forest elf **hat**

(cut one)

(back of head)

(center of head)

INDEX

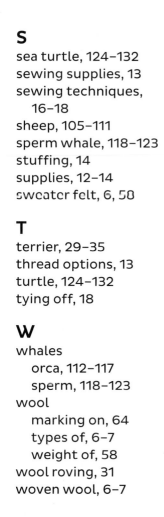